LIBERTY SHIPS EASTWARD

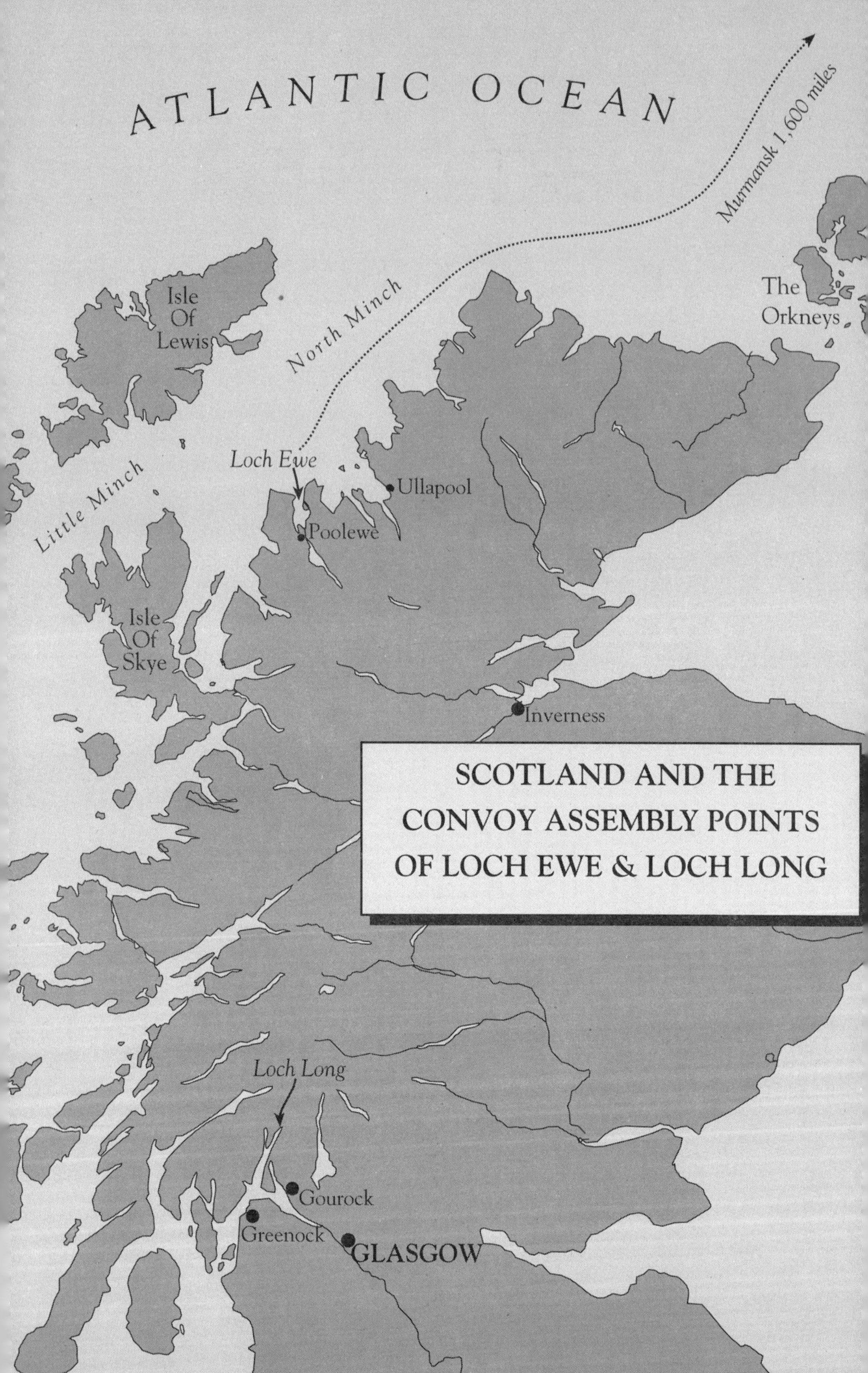
ATLANTIC OCEAN
Murmansk 1,600 miles
The Orkneys
Isle Of Lewis
North Minch
Little Minch
Loch Ewe
Ullapool
Poolewe
Isle Of Skye
Inverness
SCOTLAND AND THE CONVOY ASSEMBLY POINTS OF LOCH EWE & LOCH LONG
Loch Long
Gourock
Greenock
GLASGOW

LIBERTY SHIPS EASTWARD

George Elliott

Illustrated With Drawings By The Author

THE PROVINCIAL PRESS
Cape Elizabeth, Maine

Published by:
The Provincial Press
252 Spurwink Avenue
Cape Elizabeth, ME 04107-9613

Maps by Greeley's Mills Cartography

ISBN 0-931675-02-2

Elliott, George.
Liberty ships eastward / George Elliott.
p. cm.
Includes bibliographical references and index.
ISBN 0-931675-02-2
1. Elliott, George. 2. World War, 1939-1945—Naval operations, American. 3. Merchant marine—United States—History—20th century. 4. World War, 1939-1945—Personal narratives, American. 5. Liberty ships. 6.Sailors—United States—Biography. 7. Merchant marine -United States—Biography. I. Title.
D810.T8E43 1995
940.54'5973—dc20

95-42722
CIP

Printed In The United States Of America

DEDICATED TO

My Connie,
whose name appears
throughout this account

Introduction

Merchant seamen manning cargo vessels during World War II had a greater chance of being killed than any other servicemen in the U.S. Armed Forces. The heavy casualties and destruction of ships operating under the Merchant Marine went unpublicized throughout the war for reasons of moral and security.

"I hold no branch in higher esteem than the Merchant Marine services", declared Gen. Douglas MacArthur. During a six month period in 1942 German submarines sank nearly 400 ships in American coastal waters. In all 733 merchant ships were sunk with 6,507 merchant seamen killed in action and 4,780 missing and presumed dead. Of 713 Allied cargo ships sent to North Russia, 98 were sunk en route. Most of these statistics were kept secret until after the war. The public really never knew the facts.

Liberty ships played a major role in our eventual winning of the war. They were 10,000 ton "Ugly Ducklings," according to President Roosevelt. Another writer referred to them as having been "built by the mile and cut off by the yard."

Liberty's could be built for a minimum cost (a little over a million each) and could be produced quickly. They were uncomplicated to operate and maintain.

A total of 2,710 Libertys slid down the ways of eighteen shipyards from Maine to California. More than 200 Libertys were lost during the war. Today, two Liberty ships the *Jeremiah O'Brien* and the *John W. Brown*, remain afloat, roam the oceans as museum ships.

Those who manned the Liberty's had great regard for their dependability and durability even though they were slow and spartan. The overwhelming build up in Europe and the Pacific would not have been possible without the workhorse Liberty ships that were produced from 1940 through 1945.

George Elliott
Waterford, Maine
December, 1995

CONTENTS

Chapter One

The Maturing Of A Seaman

I stood at the engine room throttle feeling very insignificant. I had just arrived by water taxi at four p.m., and at eight p.m. I was standing my first watch as a licensed third engineer. The ship was a cargo vessel at anchorage at Newport News, Virginia, amidst many other similar vessels. It was December 7, 1943. I had barely time to find my assigned cabin when I was informed the ship would get underway on my watch. My heart sank.

I had just graduated from the Maine Maritime Academy ten days previously. During my one-week leave period, I became engaged to Connie Canning, my high school girl friend. I left Portland and reported to Boston for assignment. They ticketed me to Norfolk and within hours I was directed to the S. S. *Justin Morrill*, an almost fully loaded Liberty ship with special compartmentation for six hundred troops. I had little opportunity to look around or become acquainted with my responsibilities. Suddenly the engine room telegraph signaled "Stand by."

I had been positioned at the throttle, rocking the engine to prevent condensation from building up in the cylinders, feeling very inadequate. The thirty-six month program at the academy had been reduced to sixteen months and the engineering shop contained one inoperative steam engine salvaged from a sunken tugboat, two lathes and one milling machine. Our two required cruises of three months each on Long Island Sound hardly gave us a chance for real boning-up on steam plant operation. Most of our schedule was bookwork and lectures that centered on steam turbines and diesel engines.

Here I was standing at the base of a three-story high, "up and down" reciprocating steam engine. Its size was intimidating. I felt ill-prepared. The hot smell of steam mixed with the odor of oil heightened my anxiety as I glanced around the engine room. The sounds of the machinery all around me made me realize the weight of my new responsibility. I could sense my heart pounding above the noise. I was a scant eighteen years old. My confidence was at a low level ... very low.

Looking toward the boiler room, I saw a tall, gaunt individual with his arms crossed on his chest. He was my fireman on watch. He looked to be at least fifty. We hardly had time to exchange a hello. My second watchstander was a small, wiry fellow, also in his fifties. He barely tipped the scale at 100 pounds. Both would prove to be radical, lifelong sailors. Shorty was my oiler on watch and his duty was to circulate every half hour oiling and checking all the machinery. The third person on my watch was a utility, clean-up individual. He was a Portugese national who barely spoke English. He also was much older than I.

The engine room telegraph shattered my thoughts. "Half astern," it ordered. I clutched the reversing engine lever and opened the throttle wheel. The crankshaft came alive and the vibration became noticeable as the propeller bit into the water. We were moving. During the next hours, we constantly changed speed. Changes came on top of one another: "Half ahead, full ahead, one-third astern"—there was no let up. Finally, as our watch period was ending, the telegraph rang "Finished with engine." We had transited the harbor and were alongside a Norfolk pier. I went topside with a sense of satisfaction. I had survived. Everything had gone all right.

The pier was filled with activity. There were lines of military people with duffle bags and foot lockers, and a Salvation Army van was serving hot coffee and sandwiches as groups broke ranks in an orderly fashion. As soon as the gangway was in position, they commenced filing on board. They were sober and quiet as they boarded and were probably thinking of home as I was. In the dim light of the pier I tried to search their faces. They were young guys for the most part. There were few smiles. There were few smiles. I watched 550 Air Force men of a heavy bombardment group troop on board and disappear into the cavernous forward cargo hold. At 1 a.m., I went to my cabin, too tired to unpack, and turned in. It had been a momentous day for me.

The next morning at breakfast I met more of the ship's officers. They were all my seniors by fifteen or more years. The captain appeared to be a stern, withdrawn person, white-haired and very wrinkled. The chief engineer arrived and sat with the captain. He was a robust and loud man. He had previously been a valve salesman and had renewed his license after twelve years ashore. A rumor indicated we would be sailing during the early evening—on my watch. A twinge of discomfort struck me.

I spent most of the day inspecting the engine room and the rest of the ship, while supplies, water and fuel came on board. The *Morrill* was a west coast-built Liberty ship. This was her second voyage. She was fully loaded with cargo ranging from ammunition and aircraft bombs to general cargo, canned goods, bagged wheat and an Air Force bomber group. The forward hold had been rebuilt with five-high bunks and special ventilation. A head had been constructed on one side of the hatch cover and steam tables for mess on the other side. A medical facility was fabricated from plywood with several spaces for doctors and a small ward for patients. It was rather crowded and dismal. At the stern, other quarters housed our naval armed guard, who numbered over twenty. They manned our cannons and twenty-mm guns. The armed guard officer and seven air corps officers joined us for meals. The naval gun crew ate in a small separate area from the ship's crew.

The captain's convoy conference was held at ten a.m. and captains and armed guard officers from all ships scheduled to join in convoy met at the naval base for instructions, charts and codes. During the day frenzied activity prepared the ship for departure. A fuel barge topped off our tanks. Water tanks were filled and last minute provisions were hurried aboard. I unpacked my gear and sat down to write final letters to my folks and to Connie.

Participants in the captain's conference returned to the ship and the gangway was hauled aboard. I went below to begin my second watch. The engine didn't look quite as formidable. The engine room telegraph was set on "Stand by," as I relieved the first assistant engineer. Within moments it signaled "Half astern," and we left the pier and crossed through a glut of anchored ships.

Speed changes were rapid as we departed the harbor, passed through the submarine nets and began forming into a convoy. I went topsides when my watch ended and there was a cool overcast to chill my sweat-drenched shirt. A gentle roll was developing as we entered open water. My eyes adjusted to the darkness and I became aware of all of the ships around us.

The convoy stretched in every direction. It was an awesome sight as wakes glistening with phosphorus trailed behind the nearest vessels. Off in the dim distance, escorting destroyers were sweeping our advance as the convoy began zig-zagging. It was at this moment that the full impact of our mission sank in. We were heading into troubled waters.

We learned our destination was Oran, Algeria. I was becoming part of the war. The quiet was broken only by the sound of the wind and swish of the waves—and the muted vibration of the engine. The darkened ships seemed ghostly. I stood at the rail reflecting on the past few days and how my life had changed.

The first days at sea were blustery and rough, turning gradually to warm and sunny. Our insular midshipman training cruises had not prepared me for the clear turquoise water and rolling motion of the deep ocean. I had settled into the shipboard routine and had rapidly become accustomed to my engineering responsibilities and my new life.

The spring of 1943 was the heyday of German submarine activity. Hundreds of ships were sunk. The vital lifeline to England was nearly severed. Convoy protection was primitive and sparse. It was only now that radar and sonar equipment were becoming part of the escorts' eyes and ears. The invasion of North Africa had succeeded and the Allies had quickly overrun Sicily and were gaining a foothold in Italy at Salerno. The fighting had been bloody and fierce. Each day we were called out for fire drills, boat drills and action drills. Yet, each day passed tranquilly with calm seas and warm weather. It was deceptively quiet. The convoy plodded along at eight to nine knots. The gentle motion of the ship in the relatively calm sea made the war somewhat unreal.

I became better acquainted with my older shipmates, singling out several with whom I could become friendly. The second mate, recently a postman, and the first mate, who had been a mid-level executive with the New York Telephone Company, became my closest friends. They were in their forties and both had failed to qualify for the Navy. They were Irish as Irish could be. They called me "the Kid."

I became aware that the officers and crew on these wartime ships could be grouped into four categories. There were those professional seamen who had endured the privations of pre-war, tough times. Generally, they were cynical, radical loners with few ties ashore. A second group were former, short-time sailors who had established jobs and roots ashore. The war had brought them back to sea as they renewed and upgraded their papers. They wanted to do their part in the effort and this was a chance for a new adventure. The third group could be defined as those who wished to avoid the Army. They volunteered in the Maritime Service two steps ahead of the draft board. Good pay, three meals a day and a bunk in which to sleep helped to make their decision. Generally they were commercial fishermen, small boat sailors, shipyard workers and yachtsmen with salt water instincts.

Then there was my group, few at first. We were the new bunch coming out of the schools and academies, the ones being trained to man the ships of the accelerated, ship building program. We were the young upstarts who incurred the hostility of the other three groups in the early days. The first several weeks were an adjustment period as each group learned to accept one another. Durable, lasting friendships were seldom formed.

Watch schedules and limited social opportunities, except mealtimes, dampened any strong bonds. We also realized that when the trip ended, we would all scatter. A few would remain on that ship. Most would head home to wives and girl friends for a short leave, and then sign on another ship for the next trip.

The monotony of shipboard existence left little to do except sleep, eat and stand watch. One day was like another. I spent much of my off duty time writing to Connie, who had just entered a three year nurses' program at the Maine General Hospital.

During my high school days, when I first became attracted to Connie, war had become a sobering possibility. Gathering clouds of conflict were more and more apparent. My thoughts of art school gradually gave way to reality. A new nautical school was about to be established in Castine, Maine. With my parents' approval, I applied for admission. In spite of my lack of math credits, I was accepted for the spring class. Pearl Harbor occurred a month later.

I graduated from high school and the next day was en route

to the new Maine Maritime Academy. The war was then at its early, grimmest period. Rationing, censorship, blackouts and shortages were causing major adjustments. Two hundred eighty young men were cloistered for accelerated training in Castine, a remote small town on coastal Maine. Our accommodations and training devices were Spartan. As I sat in my cabin thinking back, it seemed a long time ago.

Christmas Day, 1943, was a particularly lonely day. It was my first Christmas away from home. There was an attempt at holiday merriment with a good effort by the cooks to serve a turkey dinner. Liberated medical alcohol was cut with canned orange juice and a few holiday decorations were taped to the bulkhead. It was a quiet celebration. Conversations were short and muted. I wandered out on deck. The sun was warm. The sea was subdued. The sky was clear except for clusters of puffy clouds. It was very un-Christmas-like for me as we steamed east, having traveled 2,850 miles from Norfolk. Every ship in the convoy was sharp and distinct in the clear air as I turned to go to my cabin to write a long and thoughtful letter. The main deck was crowded with bored and homesick Air Force men, soaking up the sun and balmy weather.

Our crossing of the Atlantic was very uneventful. Only once was there a flurry of activity and "General quarters." Nothing came of it.

Nearing Gibraltar, the seventy-two- ship convoy was signaled to slow to four knots and steam in a circle. It was reported that the enemy was deploying a number of their Norwegian and Bay of Biscay-based submarines toward the Mediterranean. We were to stay in position until additional escorts joined us.

The sudden reminder of submarines caused me to recall the cold, overcast day at Castine months before when the academy was alerted that the military had sealed off all roads leading to the coast. An enemy U-boat had landed saboteurs on the East Coast. The entire coast north and south of Castine had been cordoned. Truckloads of troops were involved. Soon after darkness, two blimps with piercing lights hovered along the shoreline. We watched them slowly cruise by and return a few hours later. The dormitory buzzed with excitement. The next morning, the milk and food supply trucks failed to arrive. Traffic was not allowed either way. On the second evening, the blimps returned. During the day patrol aircraft could be seen in the hazy overcast. That day, provision trucks arrived as roadblocks were relaxed. Later we learned that four Germans were apprehended in New York City and were charged as spies. This was a momentous event for isolated midshipmen in sleepy, coastal Castine.

Now the threat of enemy submarines was real. Tension crept into our thoughts as the convoy ceased advancing toward Gibraltar.

Following a day and a half of slowly steaming in a circle, additional escorts became visible on the horizon. We picked up speed and headed for Gibraltar in four columns. A small group peeled off with several escorts and set course for Casablanca. The main body entered the Strait of Gibraltar just as the sun was disappearing into the western ocean. Barrage balloons were sent aloft at varying heights from each ship as a deterrent against low-flying aircraft. We were at general quarters with life jackets and helmets. Looking aft we saw a spectacular sunset with the silhouette of Gibraltar on the right side and the African coast on the left. High in the distant sky was a speck of an aircraft identified as enemy. Anxiety gripped us all.

We watched as it slowly shadowed us. A nervous gunner on one of the ships triggered a burst from a twenty- mm gun. Instantaneously, guns began barking from all sides and the darkening skies were lit up with tracer bullets from all directions. Barrage balloons fell in flames and the enemy reconnaisance plane, well out of range, slipped into the night. I was not the only one who crawled into bed that night with apprehension.

We arrived at Oran and dropped anchor outside the breakwater, awaiting further orders. Sea watches were suspended and the main engine and one boiler were shut down. It was our first relaxation in more than three weeks. All took advantage of this respite. The next day I had the opportunity to go ashore for mail while the captain's conference was taking place. The trip across the bay in one of our lifeboats was a pleasant change. The short time spent in Oran left me vague memories of a hot, smelly and strange city.

Back on the *Justin Morrill*, as I devoured my newly arrived mail, word came to light-off the idle boiler. We would be making up into a smaller convoy, and heading for Port Augusta, Sicily. As we left Oran, low scudding clouds were rolling out of the north. As we maneuvered into formation, the wind strengthened and the waves mounted. During the night we endured a quickened and intensified rolling as the sea built up. The ship was snapped from side to side from the short interval between waves. It was a violent motion to experience after the slow roll in the Atlantic.

The following morning the convoy began encountering mines broken loose from an Italian minefield to the north. These ugly hazards were not easily spotted in the sea chop. During the morning numerous mines were either sunk or exploded by our escorts. Those not on watch, along with the idle airmen, became interested spectators to this show. Without warning, a stray mine appeared, nearing our port side. The wind forced it closer to the hull. The captain stopped the engine. The convoy continued, leaving one escort to remain near us.

The mine continued to drift toward us. When it was only a dozen feet away, the captain rang up "Full astern." Vibration was felt throughout the ship as the propeller began churning the water. A plume of agitated water curled along our hull, caught the mine

and gently nudged it forward, as the ship gradually moved astern. All eyes were focused on the mine as it slid past our bow, barely two feet away. We continued backing. The escort moved into position and with a couple of bursts, the mine exploded with a sharp concussion. Deck observers slowly dispersed.

We picked up speed and rejoined our convoy just in time to wheel around the recently liberated Island of Pantelleria and proceeded north into Port Augusta, Sicily.

We dropped anchor for three days, awaiting other ships to join us. The setting was enchanting, as we lay inside the submarine nets in the shadow of snow-capped Mount Etna. Bumboats came alongside. We dropped pails on a line over the side with a package of American cigarettes. In exchange for the cigarettes, we hauled up pails filled with fresh picked Sicilian oranges or almonds. Each day additional vessels joined us.

We got underway after sunrise, formed into convoy outside the harbor and headed north. There were pockets of German resistance still being mopped up in Sicily. Naples had been captured and enough of the devastation cleaned up to allow supply ships to start flowing in.

At noon of the day we left Port Augusta, we approached the narrow Strait of Messina, separating Italy and Sicily. A German spotter plane followed us. We had an eerie feeling as we watched that distant aircraft. Guns were manned and ready. Conversation was muted. The air was still.

On our port side was Sicily and the town of Messina carved into the cliffs. Graffiti was scribbled on bullet-pocked walls. Rubble filled the streets. On our starboard side was the Italian mainland. We passed through the Strait of Messina in two columns. The ocean was mirror calm and the reflection of the cliffs on each side made the passage a scenic adventure. During the evening we saw the Island of Stromboli with its continuous lava flow silhouetted on the horizon. Later, Capri was visible.

We dropped anchor outside the breakwater of Naples, Italy, well after dark on January 11. The next morning, with pilot

aboard, we steamed through the sub nets and berthed alongside a sunken Greek cargo ship that had rolled on her side after being scuttled by the Germans. At least twenty ships were sunk to obstruct the harbor. A large French passenger liner had been sunk at the main harbor pier, and many other vessels lay at right angles to the waterfront quay with decks awash.

The destruction was complete throughout the port area. Gantry cranes and waterfront facilities had been destroyed by the retiring Germans. All the buildings facing the harbor had been dynamited so that they gaped grotesquely. Four and five story buildings lay open and bare as if a huge meat cleaver had cut them in half. Curtains flapped in the breeze; toilets hung precariously with bent and twisted plumbing; beds and bedsprings were hanging from collapsed floors. Exposed interior walls of various colors created a checkerboard effect from building to building. Everywhere, one saw nothing but utter destruction. Anti-aircraft emplacements dotted the waterfront and Army vehicles resembled ants coming and going on various missions.

Wooden, bridge-like structures had been constructed over the sunken hulks along the harbor quay. Army trucks backed out on these temporary wooden bridges alongside us. Using our ship's winches and booms, pallets and slings of cargo were loaded into trucks. When loaded, these trucks drove away and others backed down for their turn. We were alongside this wooden bridge affair only a short time and then were shifted to the inner harbor anchorage near the breakwater until the next day.

Our Army Air Force people had been on board for more than a month in dank, dark holds. They had little space to lie down and were limited to little exercise. Each day seemed endless. Monotony followed boredom, and seasickness came easily. Their anxiety to disembark from the *Morrill* was intense. We sympathized with them.

At mid-afternoon, we got underway on a northerly heading. After traveling in convoy, we felt very vulnerable steaming alone. Our destination was a small harbor just north of Naples. We arrived in the early evening at Pozzuoli and dropped anchor amid seven other cargo ships.

The following afternoon, Navy LCI's came alongside and our Air Corps guys finally began disembarking down rope ladders. Their supplies and equipment were loaded into a larger LST. We stood on deck watching this activity with interest. As we watched, I suddenly recognized one of the Navy boat coxswains as Bill Nisbet, a fellow Deering High School graduate. I waved him to come up. He left his boat well secured with another Navy fellow and scrambled up one of the rope ladders.

He was delighted to see me and we went to my cabin. It would take another hour to load his boat and have it ready to return to shore. We talked, joked and had a lively conversation.

Just before leaving, he became serious and asked me for a favor. Would I make it a point to visit his parents when I got back to Portland? I responded that I certainly would and asked him why. His answer caught me speechless for a moment. He said he wouldn't be returning home. I asked what he meant. He said he had a premonition that he would never see Portland again. He was not dramatic about it—just matter-of-fact. However, there was no mistaking his seriousness.

S.S. Justin Morrill
Naples, Italy
January, 1944

The Air Force group finished disembarking and the LCI's started toward shore. We learned they were on their way to the heavy bomber base at Bari, Italy, on the opposite coast. I waved goodbye to my high school friend and watched the little fleet cross the harbor in the growing twilight.

The next morning I discovered we were the only ship left in the harbor. The others had departed during the night. At noon we were directed back to Naples to the same spot alongside the hulk of the Greek cargo vessel where we had been before. Immediately the hatches were uncovered and cargo was unloaded in earnest. It was noise and hubbub twenty-four hours a day, with winches whirring and trucks backing into position opposite our hatches. We had an opportunity to go ashore, but could not leave the harbor area. It was sealed off because of a typhus outbreak. The authorities were attempting to separate military personnel from the civilian population. We saw a number of stations where the Italian dock workers were dusted with DDT to limit the typhus spread. After all our walking, we saw little except destruction, rubble and Army activity.

We were drawn to the main pier that jutted out into the harbor. Pre-war Mediterranean cruise ships tied up here. The pier was a storage point for thousands of bombs, piled row by row, like cordwood. Along the harborside quay, small arms ammunition was stacked and Army trucks constantly moved cargo. Army, self-propelled, railroad derricks unloaded tanks and trucks. Activity was intense everywhere. Ships unloading; vehicular traffic hustling here and there; battalions of Army guys working day and night, unloading, unloading and unloading.

During the day, two Army troop transports arrived and disembarked troops fresh from the U. S. and a radio bulletin reported our poorly planned Allied landing at Anzio, just north of Naples.

I thought many times that the people back home had no idea what war was really like. Here I was amid an unbelievable amount of war provisions, equipment and activity, surrounded by blocks of gutted buildings and a harbor strewn with capsized vessels. The ravage of war was difficult to describe. Censorship prevented my relating what I had seen.

Our fourth night of unloading was interrupted by an air raid. Sirens sounded and the whole harborside and docked ships went on full alert. The greatest fireworks I had ever seen burst forth overhead as thousands of tracer bullets were fired skyward. The display was awesome and the sounds deafening. The whole sky was alive with white and red tracers. Searchlights swept the sky from many locations and appeared to dance to and fro. It was a fascinating show.

Four bombers, each with two bombs, managed to overfly the harbor at a high altitude. Greeted by an overwhelming barrage of anti-aircraft fire, they jettisoned their loads. All bombs

Friday, JANUARY 7 ~~February 4~~, 1944
35th Day—331 Days to Follow
39960 32 (24)

PASSED MALTA LAST NIGHT, AND HEADED NORTH. ARRIVED IN PORT AUGUSTA BAY SICILY THIS MORNING, AND DROPPED ANCHOR. ABOUT FORTY OTHER SHIPS IN HERE WITH US TODAY. PORT AUGUSTA IS MORE OF A TOWN THAN CITY, AND HAS NO DOCKS, THE HOUSES ARE ALL CEMENTED, OR MUD. IT IS QUITE HILLY, AND WELL FORESTED. BARRAGE BALLOONS FILL THE SKY, AND THERE ARE SEVERAL WARSHIPS WITH US. STILL NO ORDERS, AND STILL THE ARMY IS ON BOARD. HAD A BAD WATCH THIS MORNING, MANEAUVERING THROUGH MINEFIELDS, AND SUBMARINE NETS. I THINK I DID WELL, CONSIDERING. WEATHER MUCH COOLER, BUT STILL NICE. PORT AUGUSTA WAS HEAVILY BOMBED SIX DAYS AGO, AND I AM REALLY SURPRISED NOW.

Saturday, JANUARY 8 ~~February 5~~, 1944
36th Day—330 Days to Follow
418.28 + 5.00 = 423.28 33 1

STOOD FROM MIDNITE TO 8 PORT WATCH. SAW THE SUNRISE, AND SAW THE MOST BEAUTIFUL SIGHT AS, SUN HIT FAMOUS MOUNT ETNA. IT IS INTERESTING TO SEE THE SMALL SAILBOATS COME OUT TO US, TYPICAL OF THEIR COUNTRY. THE BUMBOATS WERE AROUND TODAY SWAPPING ORANGES AND PECANS FOR AMERICAN CIGARETTES. DELICIOUS, JUICY ORANGES. THE TOWN IS WELL BOMBED, AND THERE ARE SEVEN VISIBLE SUNK SHIPS.

Sunday, JANUARY 9 ~~February 6~~, 1944
37th Day—329 Days to Follow
441.56 + 10 = 451.56 34 2

STOOD FROM 8 THIS MORNING TO 4 THIS AFTERNOON. GOT ENGINES READY TWICE BUT DIDN'T MOVE BECAUSE OF CHANGE OF ORDERS. PLAYED FOUR HANDED CRIBBAGE WITH THE NAVAL OFFICERS LAST NIGHT, AND HAD A COKE.

Two pages from the diary the author kept while on convoy duty.

dropped harmlessly in the harbor, except one. It struck the Liberty ship at the quay alongside us and penetrated dead center down the smokestack. It exploded three decks below. Three officers and eighteen of the ship's crew survived. Luckily, they were standing on the quay. Everyone in the deckhouse was killed.

From our vantage point, the deckhouse and ship appeared to be hardly damaged. Internally, it was gutted. Bulkheads were bulged out; decks dished and ripped; nothing was left of the galley or crew's quarters. The fire room and engine room were badly damaged. This particular vessel had just returned alongside us from the Anzio invasion. She had discharged her cargo and troops while under constant air attack there, and had been credited with shooting down one plane and probably two others.

When we went to look more closely at the damage to the S. S. *William Mullholland*, we saw a sight one never forgets. The seam in the rear corner of the deckhouse had been blown open and through the open gash, the second mate could be seen, burned to death. The boiler uptakes were in shambles, and broken steam pipes still emitted wisps of steam. Boiler casings were blown off, exposing the steam generating tubes like a skeleton.

We watched an American destroyer towed into the harbor. She had hit a mine and her machinery spaces were laid open. Another vivid memory was the arrival of survivors of a British hospital ship. Although clearly marked and with all lights on, the hospital ship had been hit with a German radio-controlled bomb. She suffered many casualities and had been part of the Anzio invasion force. That's where the other seven ships went from our anchorage at Pozzuoli. The unfortunate *Mullholland* was one of those ships.

Barrage balloons were used extensively as a low-level aircraft defense in Naples. They were attached to Navy launches which continuously moved about the harbor area. Depth charges were dropped periodically within the harbor as a defense against underwater swimmers or manned torpedoes. The Italians were noted for their skill in this underwater form of attack. All day and night, we heard these loud depth-charge explosions. They were dropped at random in different locations. When dropped nearby, the ship was severely jolted from the underwater concussion. Sleep became a luxury.

I watched Italian women picking between the cobble-stones of the street, trying to recover grains of wheat which had spilled from broken wheat sacks. Food was in extremely short supply during this period. It was pitiful to witness the degradation people suffered.

The weather was ideal during our stay in Naples. The temperature was comfortable and mornings were clear and pleasant. Humidity and haze could be counted on each afternoon. The Bay of Naples was impressive, with Vesuvius the focal point to the south. Air raid warnings with screeching sirens occurred several nights, but nothing developed except the spectacular fireworks display of anti-aircraft gunnery. During the days, waves of our own B-17 bombers formed overhead as they ventured north to break the German resistance. The beachhead at Anzio was not easily established and tough fighting was taking place there.

Finally, we were unloaded and a small contingent of Italian P.O.W.'s were escorted on board, guarded by Army M.P.'s, for our homebound trip. Within a short period, we made up into a small convoy and headed south on Lincoln's Birthday.

Mail arrived for us in Sicily. Among the many letters from Connie, my folks, brothers and sister, was one that informed me that my Navy coxswain friend, Bill Nisbet, was officially listed as missing in action. It was difficult to believe. He had visited me just days before in my cabin. His premonition haunted me.

Two of my eight to twelve watch-standers were avowed Communists. Shorty, my oiler, and toothless Slim, my fireman, were bitter, pre-war, depression sea dogs. They spent many watch hours leaning on the log desk, railing against the capitalist system and bitterly denouncing the Mellens, Rockefellers, and Fords. They burned my ears endlessly about their philosophy. From them, I learned of the tough conditions and tough times on the depression-years' ships. They had been hardened under austere conditions and difficult times. In spite of their radical beliefs, I liked them both. Neither had any family or roots ashore. They were union sailors through and through and were finally earning decent wages, eating wholesome food and sleeping in clean quarters.

Our small convoy proceeded from Port Augusta, Sicily, back to Oran, North Africa. More mail met us in Oran. Letters from both Connie and my folks informed me that my Navy friend was now officially listed as killed in action. He was manning his LCI with a load of fully equipped infantrymen during the first wave at Anzio and had struck a mine. None had survived. Now I had an additional burden of what to say when I visited his folks in Portland. He was an only son.

The return crossing in a large 120-ship convoy was very rough but uneventful. The *Justin Morrill* was signaled to peel off the convoy with two other ships to berth in Baltimore. We tied up in the late afternoon of March 19, 1944. It took two hours to get through by phone to Connie. When I finally reached her, we talked endlessly. Hearing her voice after all these weeks was electrifying and delightful. I called from the Lord Baltimore Hotel, which was crawling with servicemen. I went to the dining room to enjoy fresh cold milk and a Maine lobster. The lack of fresh milk for these many weeks was a substantial privation for me. Returning to the lobby, I learned that all rooms were booked. I spent the night sleeping in a lounge chair, while many other servicepeople slept on sofas and the floor. It was wartime.

My first ship was an experience that matured my outlook rapidly, even though I didn't have enough beard to shave. I was the youngest crew member on board, not counting the Navy gun crew. I now had a stripe and a half on my sleeve and was authorized to wear two ribbons on my jacket. Big battles were happening on both land and sea in the Pacific as the Mediterranean area was cooling down and the Atlantic was gradually being controlled.

I found Portland awash with Navy people and shipyard workers when I arrived home. The North Atlantic Fleet was based in Casco Bay and numerous warships anchored there on any given day. Two shipyards in South Portland turned out Liberty ships and employed up to 40,000 people on three shifts. War activity was everywhere. Nightly blackouts, gas and food rationing were an accepted part of life. The tide of the Atlantic war was just beginning to shift to our advantage.

Most of my leave was spent with Connie when she was off duty from the hospital. I began to pressure her to get married. I also sat for my second engineer's license and found the courage to visit the parents of my Navy coxswain friend who was killed at Anzio. It was a difficult chore for me.

Chapter Two

Nosebleeds, Morals & Injuries

My next ship, in May 1944, was the S. S. *George Eldridge*, a brand new Liberty just built at the South Portland yards. We loaded in Portland, steamed to Boston and joined a fourteen-ship coastwise convoy to Halifax. Three days later we made up into a large Britain-bound convoy of 138 ships. Our escorts included two converted tanker aircraft carriers. Fifteen more ships joined the convoy the next day, making 153 ships—the largest convoy ever formed.

Three days out, we ran into a huge Atlantic storm. I came up from my engine watch and witnessed a Liberty ship, two columns away, break in two. The bow section broke away just forward of the deckhouse and pivoted sideways at an angle, as the rest of the ship moved forward. Within minutes, the bow section sank. The aft section and deckhouse remained afloat. The remaining hull slowed down and stopped. The convoy moved on, with an escort standing by the crippled ship. We understood lat-

er than an oceangoing tug from Halifax was able to haul it back to port. There were no casualties. Two reasons were given for these Liberty ship break-ups: the west coast all-welded method of shipbuilding and improper cargo loading.

This convoy was massive. It stretched from horizon to horizon. We were heavily loaded, with deck cargo covering the main deck. Wooden crates of gliders were shackled to the deck. Our cargo was crated aircraft engines, army trucks, Sherman tanks and ammunition. A Navy blimp patrolled above us the first day and a half out.

Prewar British biplanes were exposed on the small flight decks of the mini-carriers. When definite threats of U-boat activity existed, they launched these antiquated aircraft to patrol the convoy. Each plane carried smoke bombs to mark any suspected U-boat location. Two open cockpits held a pilot and an observer. They were ideal planes for convoy spotting because they were so slow they could practically hover between columns of ships. As they flew up through our column, you could look down into their cockpit. Nearing the United Kingdom, more escorts joined us and the convoy was broken into smaller convoy groups. Our section was destined for Glasgow. We formed into a single column and entered the Clyde Estuary.

Shipboard routine is a lonely existence. The absence of fem-

9

S.S. George Eldridge
Atlantic - May 1944

ininity magnified the aloneness. Everything aboard a ship is masculine. The lack of curtains at the portholes and omission of braided rugs on the deck, and even the plain unimaginative bed covering, reminded us how we missed femininity. In my state of mind, the loneliness of the times weighed heavily. I wasn't homesick, but was acutely aware of being alone much of the time. I was, up to this time, the youngest licensed officer. The nearest person to my age was in his thirties. Once again, I was the babe amidst older men. Even the crew on my watch were twenty to forty years my senior.

His name, Marion, seemed odd to me. It was a girl's name where I came from. I learned it was not an uncommon name in the south. He had a thick, Alabama accent and had been a shoe salesman until his draft number came up. He quickly opted for the Merchant Marine, and following a short period of training, came on board as the ship's purser.

A cheerful sort of person in his early thirties, he rapidly became the humorist and entertainer during the trip. As purser, he handled most of the ship's business, as well as being the first-aid medical person for minor sicknesses and injuries. He operated the ship's "slop chest," which was a basic store for cigarettes, candy, razor blades and work clothes. Marion could be counted on to bring a smile during dull periods, or a chuckle amid tense moments. His jocular personality often relieved our shipboard monotony. Even during his periods of seasickness he managed to be upbeat and optimistic. I found myself drawn to him. His outlook was a tonic for my spirits and during idle times, I felt comfortable "chinning" with him.

His southern accent generated many hours of interesting discussions between us. Marion and I hit it off great during the trip. It became a case of a down-Easter and a southerner finding mutual ground. We became good temporary shipboard friends. Wartime conditions were a great equalizer.

One of the memorable pleasures that sparked my monastic life was coming from the engine room after my midnight to four a.m. stretch and smelling freshly baked bread. Such a beautiful aroma! I went into the galley, picked up a loaf of hot bread fresh out of the oven, grabbed a quarter pound of butter and headed for my cabin.

Nosebleeds were a fairly common occurrence for me and were a nuisance all through my school years. Sometimes they became quite severe, often bad enough for me to be sent home from school. If I sneezed or simply bent over, my nose would begin bleeding. This tendency continued aboard ship. One particular experience was very unnerving.

The fellow who came to wake me for my engine room watch turned on the light, took one look at me and hustled out of my cabin to awaken the captain and other officers. When I awoke, five faces were staring down at me. My head was stuck to the pillow and my face was caked with blood. While sleeping, I had developed a nosebleed. When the watch-stander came to wake me, he found me thoroughly bloodied. The pillow, sheets and bed were saturated. His eyes told him that someone had bashed in my skull. He went for help. By the time I cleaned up and got dressed to stand watch, I realized how weak I was. I had lost a large quantity of blood. It was several days before I regained my strength. Days later, I found dried blood on the deck under my mattress and box springs.

A convoy commodore controlled the merchant ships. He usually took up quarters in the lead ship. The escorts were controlled through the escort commander. Normally, a smaller merchant-type vessel was equipped as the rescue ship and carried medical personnel and rescue devices.

Foreign flag vessels were usually the slower, older, coal-burning steamers. They released clouds of telltale smoke as they maintained steam to keep station in the convoy. We looked upon these foreigners with disdain. Darkness, or fog, was welcomed since it hid their existence. Frequent breakdowns caused them to disrupt formation and lag behind the convoy. This created another responsibility for the escorting destroyers. On clear days, coal burners made us shudder as we watched their trails of smoke drifting toward the horizon ... a visible invitation to the enemy.

As the war progressed, more and more Liberty ships made up a large share of the convoys and the slower coal-burning foreign ships were gradually segregated into their own convoys. Aircraft protection in the form of blimps and four-engined Liberators and Catalina flying boats were more available on both sides of the Atlantic. They substantially reduced the submarine threat when we were within their patrolling radius.

By war's end, Liberty ships were the predominant ships in most convoys and in most harbors, along with the newer, more sophisticated foreign diesels and turbine ships.

Due to their simple basic design, Liberty ships were able to sustain severe damage and still remain operable. Such resilience allowed many Libertys and their crews to return to safety for another day.

Censorship was a nettlesome wartime necessity. The armed guard officer was normally the shipboard censor, which tended to taint his relationship with others to a small extent. Writing letters became an art. Mentioning a sightseeing trip to Vesuvius would be excised, or noting that you hoped to see someone on Monday would be struck out because that would indicate an arrival time of the ship. Many thoughts were rendered unintelligible with either black ink or razor cut. Both incoming and outgoing mail suffered the indignity of censorship.

We arrived at Gourock, Scotland, and anchored for three hours and were then shifted upriver to Glasgow. It was a tight squeeze between ships, but they moved us into the dock area and began immediately unloading our deck cargo and Sherman tanks.

The next day, ammunition and cargo were unloaded from our lower holds.

I discovered that the morals in Europe were different from my puritanical, New England upbringing. My exploration of downtown Glasgow took place in the evening. The purser and I went sightseeing along the blacked-out main street. Elevated railroad overpasses crisscrossed the main artery and numerous closed shops lined both sides of the darkened street. The doorway to each shop was occupied with two people making love. It was both shocking and amusing to us. Our upbringing caused us to be surprised; our nature caused us to be amused.

On another occasion, the two of us met a couple of local girls at a U.S.O. and invited them to dinner and the theater. Halfway through the movie, I felt a hand on my knee which startled me. It soon started traveling north. That shook me. I rose to go to the men's room and my buddy also left. His girl was doing the same maneuver. We both decided it was time to leave.

We returned from Glasgow to Gourock one dark evening by train. British railcars consist of multi-person compartments, each accessible from the station platform through its own door. We entered our compartment, along with several civilians, a British sailor and a female Wren. Soon we moved out of the well-lighted station into total darkness. You couldn't see any of the occupants in the compartment. Hushed conversation took place over the noise of the railroad and suddenly I was aware of shoeless feet bracing against my seat. My God, they were doing it right in the compartment opposite me! I couldn't believe it. I simply couldn't believe it.

When we arrived at the Gourock station and light again poured into our compartment, I studied the Wren carefully. She was composed and neatly uniformed, with both shoes on. Nothing was out of place or disarrayed. I still couldn't believe it. The British sailor was equally organized. We let them leave first and watched them go. My shipmate asked if I were aware of what had taken place. Over a cup of hot chocolate, we both recounted the unimaginable—and laughed. What a surprise for a couple of young innocents from America.

On June 6, the Allies were ashore at Normandy. The following day, the chief radio operator and I took the train to Balloch and boarded a side-wheeler excursion steamer for a day trip up legendary Loch Lomond. We met two U. S. Army nurses on board who were taking a breather from their American Field Hospital in southern England. We had a relaxed conversation as each of us unwound and felt the relief of the times. We lunched with them during a two-hour stopover at the head of the lake. They related the tension that had built up treating the severe casualities of American airmen involved in the heavy air battles over the continent. We unloaded our anxieties in turn. Our brief encounter with them was both social and therapeutic. We returned to Glasgow by train and they continued on to sourthern England. It was one of those chance meetings that had special meaning for each of us. We hardly knew their names. We returned to the S. S. *Eldridge* late in the evening. News from the Normandy invasion was guarded.

Unloading was half completed and on the 13th, we steamed back down the Clyde. We crossed the channel to Belfast, Northern Ireland, during the night, unescorted, and were put alongside the grain pier where the balance of our cargo of grain was sucked out with huge hoses. The fifteen remaining Sherman tanks were hoisted out of the hold and driven off. We imagined they were sorely needed in Normandy.

Staying in Belfast for five days, we were able to spend time ashore, enjoying the sights and reasonably good food. Fine weather favored our respite, which was unusual. Rain, mist and fog are most common there.

The news from Normandy began to reflect more optimism. We were shifted to Bangor, Northern Ireland, and remained at anchor for five more days before making up a seventy-ship convoy with vessels coming from Liverpool, as well as Glasgow. No mail had been received since our arrival in Scotland.

We headed home into a heavy sea. Apparently we were skirting the outer edge of a good old Atlantic storm. The wind was not strong, but the sea was building into sizable swells. There was low overcast and although visibility was marginal, the captain had posted a bow lookout as a precaution.

The lookout, a man in his late fifties, was a former professor at Amherst. Ineligible for the armed forces and wanting to be involved in the great struggle, he became an ordinary seaman and shipped out in the Maritime Service. As bow lookout, he was standing at the bow leaning each elbow on the bow bulwark. Directly behind him, in the deck, was the hatch cover to the paint locker. The ship was rolling and pitching in the heavy swells. An unusually heavy pitch caused the hatchcover to fall forward and pinned the lookout's legs to the deck. Both ankles were compound-fractured and he was in deep pain. He was given emergency morphine and the convoy commodore was signaled by blinker light.

We were moved to the outer edge of the convoy and directed to drop back. The rescue ship crossed through the convoy, maneuvered close by and dropped their motor whaleboat, with four men aboard, into the turbulent ocean. Our injured seaman was strapped into a wire stretcher and taken to the after cargo hatch. The steam winch was activated and the cable hooked to the stretcher. Our ship was stopped and held sideways to the waves to create less sea chop for the whaleboat, as it approached. Then began a twenty-minute, intense drama.

The injured man, firmly strapped into the stretcher, was hoisted out over the side. The whaleboat came in as close as it dared. The trick was to time the release of the winch to the moment the whaleboat was at the peak of a crest. They tried time and again. The poor guy was jerked up and down, swinging on the end of the boom. The medics in the whaleboat tried to keep themselves positioned under the boom. It was nip and tuck with each try. The boat surged up and down, ten and fifteen feet, and only four to five feet from our hull. Our ship was rolling heavily,

Lookout
S.S. George Eldridge
June - 1944

which meant the boom was also arching up and down. They almost made it a couple of times. So close, but not quite. Each bystander was imagining how the fellow in the stretcher must be reacting to this wild transfer. After many tries, everything happened flawlessly.

The whaleboat crested on a wave. The winchman dropped the cable with perfect timing and the medics in the whaleboat instantly released the cable. The stretcher was in the whaleboat with hardly a bump. Relief swept through all onlookers. The whaleboat turned and made for the relief ship, bobbing like a cork on the waves. Our engine strained as we swung about and came up to speed. We had been vulnerable and unprotected during this mid-ocean transfer and were anxious to rejoin the safety of the convoy, which had disappeared into the overcast. Submarines were known to be in the area. It took several hours to catch up and resume station. The rescue ship didn't rejoin the convoy until hours later. We never heard the fate of the college professor.

That night and the next morning were punctuated by con-

tinuous depth charging and nighttime illumination on various sides of the convoy. We had two jeep aircraft carriers with us, plus numerous corvettes and British destroyers as escorts. At dawn, aircraft were launched for observation. The sea continued to be turbulent, but visibility improved. Our zigzagging course exposed us to all kinds of wave directions.

Several recent convoys had taken a rough beating between Greenland and Labrador and their escorts were sorely pressed. The final leg of the trip was spent in two days of dense fog and then in clear, bright, warm weather with ideal sea conditions. The temperature was in the 80's and 90's, and the engine and fire rooms were 115 to 120 degrees. The full convoy could be seen and it was an impressive sight. A group of ships peeled off for Halifax while we proceeded southward to Nantucket Shoals Lightship and New York City, to be berthed at Pier 37.

Once clear of customs and immigration and paid off, I attempted to get out of New York. The airlines were booked, the bus terminals were a zoo and my only hope was the State of Maine Express leaving that evening. I slept fitfully in my Pullman berth.

I had given a great deal of thought to marriage. I returned to Maine with every intention of convincing Connie. The times were uncertain. The world was living for the moment and everything appeared right for us to seriously consider marriage. Connie, on the other hand, was determined to finish her nurse's training. She argued that it was important to her to have a profession. She was practical, while I was romantic. Her view prevailed. Down deep, I knew she was right. I also recognized that the uncertainty of the times might deny us another chance.

My thoughts went back to the day we became engaged and I had just graduated from Castine. We were waiting for a bus. It was cold and drizzly. She had completed only two weeks of her three-year nurse's training program. I was rationalizing why we should become engaged. She was quietly listening. I finally spelled out my earnest proposal just as the bus pulled up and its door popped open.

Connie folded the umbrella and we boarded the crowded bus. There was an empty seat at the rear and another in back of the driver. Connie took the seat at the rear of the bus and I looked over the driver's shoulder as the windshield wipers cleared the drizzle. I had formally asked her to marry me and the bus had delayed her response. I glanced back at her several times, but couldn't read an answer in her face. Misgivings and uncertainties dominated my thoughts. The bus stopped frequently to pick up additional passengers.

The aisle was soon filled with people and I couldn't see Connie. When we arrived intown, it was raining quite hard. I got off the bus and waited for all the other passengers to step out. Finally, Connie appeared smiling. She said "Yes." We stood in the rain for a moment and embraced, quite oblivious to others. All thoughts of uncertainties disappeared.

My seven-day break between graduation from the academy and boarding my first ship was ending. The war had become critical in both the Atlantic and the Pacific. Uncertainty and turmoil gripped all levels of society. We were now engaged to be married and our world had become impossible to predict.

A pang of nostalgia tugged at me as I recalled those precious moments. Here I was, about to leave once again. My few days at home had really resolved nothing.

On August 15, 1944, I signed on the S. S. *Edward Spafford* while she was still on the shipbuilding ways at South Portland. Two days later, I took Connie and my folks into the shipyard to watch her launching. I was able to spend a good deal of time with Connie when she was off duty. The ship was finished and we were prepared to leave. Then the fan engine shaft snapped and I had another couple of days to convince Connie, but with no results.

My sea time and license allowed me to wear two full stripes on my Maritime Service uniform and four authorized ribbons—a satisfying feeling for a nineteen-year old.

Right: Launching of a Liberty ship at the West Yard, South Portland, Maine

Shipyard Society

OBRIEN

The day before we were scheduled to leave the outfitting pier, we were informed the the *Spafford* would not be loaded in Portland, That was unusual. We got underway late in the afternoon and headed south out of Portland Harbor. We transited the Cape Cod Canal and went directly into Sullivan's Drydock in Brooklyn, New York. The trip through Long Island Sound and the East River brought back memories of my earlier school training days.

The first evidence of what was ahead of us became apparent when an additional heavy steel plate was welded to our bow. Next, a yard crew began thoroughly insulating all of the deckhouses. Navy armaments people cut loose the brand-new guns just placed on the ship at South Portland and replaced them with semi-automatic cannons. The stern deckhouse was doubled in size and a new deckhouse was fabricated on the boat deck. More twenty-mm guns were added. Additional refrigeration and food storage rooms were built. We were each issued fur vests, wool jackets, wool underwear, socks and rubber lifesaving suits. It didn't take much guessing to get the picture. We were heading for a cold climate and were being prepared for a hot reception. Northern Russia was our obvious destination.

Months earlier, New York City had become a familiar place, beginning with my first visit to the big city as a cadet-midshipman. At that time we were bussed to an abandoned rail spur between Bucksport and Castine. The antiquated passenger coaches were resurrected from some bygone era. They were wood construction with short-backed, flipover, rush seats, and there was a cast-iron stove for heat. Five of these coaches were coupled to a steam locomotive for the hot and dirty, all day trip to New York. Several times we were shunted onto a siding for long periods while regular trains made their schedules. Box lunches and drinks were given to each midshipman. At every populated area we hung out windows, waving at girls. The sight of a special train loaded with young, uniformed midshipmen caused a spontaneous reaction. People waved and shouted enthusiastically. It was a tiring trip.

We jerked into 125th Street Station at 8:30 that evening and boarded a fleet of busses for Throgs Neck. There we filed on board the *Allegheny*, an aging, Caribbean passenger vessel that had been converted to a training ship and renamed the *American Seafarer*. It was our home for the next three months as we cruised up and down Long Island Sound.

Sinkings in the Atlantic were frequent. Both training cruises were confined to the protected area of Long Island Sound. It was a rigorous, underway training program with not much spare time except on weekends. Our second training cruise, months later, took place on an old Hog Island vessel, the *American Pilot.*

Our knowledge of New York City over a six-month, two-cruise period became quite sharp. This present exposure to the Big Apple had few mysteries. New York City was a vibrant, exciting place and the war heightened the pitch of activity.

The *Edward Spafford* slipped out of dry dock and over to the Army Port of Embarkation, Pier 11, where we loaded small arms ammunition, aircraft bombs, cases of explosives, Sherman tanks, canned goods, plywood, airfield landing mats and aircraft engines. The top layer in the holds was packed with bagged grain. Special pads were welded on the main deck and gantry cranes swung eight large Baldwin railroad locomotives into position over the pad eyes which were tied down with steel cables. Next came four self-propelled railroad cranes, and finally twelve Army tanks were strapped to the deck. During our three-week drydock and loading period, the ship's galley was shut down and we had to fend for our meals ashore. Noonday hot dogs and uptown evening meals became the rule.

Our Navy armed guard came aboard to be housed in the new, enlarged stern deckhouses. There were 153 men and three officers.

We steamed out Ambrose Channel and joined a Nova Scotia-bound coastwise convoy, shadowed by two Navy blimps and a Catalina flying boat. We anchored in the inner harbor at Halifax for several days and then departed in a Britain bound convoy of 70 ships. We officially learned our destination was the Soviet Union. Upon our arrival in Scotland we would be made up into a North Russian convoy.

Our zigzagging convoy slid across the Atlantic rather uneventfully. Weather was favorable and the convoy was well-disciplined. We had several periods of sub alerts, but the resultant activity by the escorts was well ahead of us on the horizon. Course changes and periods of depth-charging kept whatever was out there away from the convoy. Sonar-equipped and-trained escorts were most effective.

We were within sight of the Scottish coast when I came up from watch in the engine room at dawn. I was hot and sweaty. The air was cool. The headlands of Scotland could be seen on the horizon and the convoy was in the process of shifting from a broad square of ships to a column, four vessels in width. As I looked out over the convoy, daydreaming, a sudden blinding flash, followed closely by a thunderous concussion, took place. I felt momentary heat on my face. Where there had been an oil tanker, now there was only a massive cloud of smoke and water spray, and chunks of metal splashing into the sea. When the smoke and spray disappeared, there was no tanker. Nothing remained. No floating debris. No sign of anything.

Ships scattered, as the few remaining escorts charged in. The rescue ship came up to the point of the explosion, but there was nothing to rescue. The convoy gradually reformed and moved on, leaving the escorts and rescue vessel at the scene. Others who had come on deck to see what had happened, returned to their stations or cabins. I went to mine and sat down, reviewing in my mind what I had seen. Suddenly, I realized if torpedoes had caused the massive explosion they probably had to pass between our stern and the ship in line behind us. The chilling truth numbed me. I can't describe how sobering that thought was.

We steamed up the Clyde to Greenock, Scotland. There we anchored midst a mass of cargo ships, troop ships and warships.

Among our crew was a cook given almost celebrity status. His function as chief cook fitted his rotund appearance. He created both respect and anxiety in the rest of us. He was a quiet person and kept to himself. We forgave his personal stockpile of ale that filled his footlocker. He did not abuse his weakness, although his cabin had the aroma of a brewery. He had gone to sea as a youth. After settling down ashore, he became a business person, raised a family, and succeeded in real estate early in his career. He owned several apartment buildings, two office buildings and other properties when the signs of impending war reawakened his dreams of coming back to sea. At fifty-five, he signed over his holdings to his wife, hired a property manager and shipped out as a cook, just prior to our entering the hostilities.

He happened to be on the S.S. *Robin Moor*, first American flagged merchant vessel to be torpedoed. He was quickly rescued by a British destroyer and flew back to New Orleans where he signed on a cargo ship bound for South Africa. Twelve days out, that ship was attacked by a U-boat and sunk. He and seven other surviviors existed for sixteen days in a lifeboat before being picked up. Following ten days' hospitalization in Brazil for severe sunburn and lesions, he shipped out on a ship that was rammed in a nighttime convoy collision and barely made it back to port. We accorded him a heroic status, but were apprehensive that he might be a formidable jinx, especially on a dangerous trip such as this. Our mixed feelings tolerated his fondness for ale. Our captain chose to look the other way. His cooking skills were unequalled.

Chapter Three
Destination: Murmansk

My mother had a very close friend who had immigrated from Scotland with her husband years before. My mother's friend urged me to look up her sister, if ever I were in Greenock again. Well, here I was. I loaded a canvas handbag with oranges, a tin of ham, a dozen eggs and some cheese, and went looking for her. I located the home of my mother's friend's sister in Greenock and identified myself. She lived in a very substantial, two and one-half-story brick home on a promontory overlooking the Clyde. I gave her my bag of goodies. She was visibly overwhelmed and pleased. She hadn't seen an orange in months and her ration of eggs was only two a month. The British supply of cheese, dairy products and hams was cut off by the German occupation of Holland.

She made tea and we sat in her front room which overlooked all the shipping in port. We talked and talked. She wanted to know everything. It was a very pleasant visit. She asked me to return the next day. The following day I arrived with two bags of grapefruit, eggs, bacon and an assortment of items no longer available to British civilians. She was delighted with my treasure. Her nephew and wife were there to meet me. He was a two-striper in the British Navy, serving on destroyers. He expressed great respect and admiration for the merchant sailors, for the risk they took. I had great respect for him as an escort sailor, tossed and buffeted trying to protect us in the convoys. We enjoyed each other for several hours before I had to return to my ship. When he learned we were heading for Russia, he shrugged and raised his eyebrows.

We swung at anchor for two days at Greenock, Scotland, with a large group of other ships, including the *Queen Mary*, *Aquitania* and various cargo vessels. The *Queen Mary* left the following day. We learned later that she was carrying Winston Churchill to meet President Roosevelt for a wartime conference. The next day we departed with twelve other vessels and sailed north around the top of Scotland, through the many isles. The trip over the top of Scotland was an unusually scenic voyage. The sights were spectacular. Our gathering place at Loch Ewe was a large isolated bay or inlet. Thirteen Russian-bound vessels were already there. Other ships arrived during the next few days.

Anxiety was building because we had all read or heard stories about the brutal "Murmansk Run." All previous convoys had taken a fearful beating from air and submarine attacks. The British were watching the German battleship, *Tirpitz*. The *Gneisenau* and *Prinz Eugen* were also poised in Norwegian fjords threatening any convoy heading north. Those formidable enemy surface vessels, plus their submarine fleet and air force based in Norway, gave the Germans heavy hitting power. The pocket battleship *Scharnhorst* was sunk earlier while attempting to intercept a previous North Russia convoy.

When Hitler invaded the Soviet Union, the British immediately laid plans for an arms supply to North Russia. The initial success the Germans reaped for their aggression soon turned into

Arnold Valcour
Detail of a model of the S.S.* Edward Spafford*, built by the author, showing crated cargo and tanks loaded on the after deck.

a bitter struggle. Raging battles on the Eastern Front began to cast doubt on the outcome. Getting desperately needed supplies to the Russians could tip the balance. American lend-lease provided the war materiel and convoys began to steam north into the Arctic. From the beginning, the Germans contested the effort vigorously. Ship losses were heavy due to the shortage of escorts. Finally, convoy PQ-17 suffered unacceptable sinkings and the Murmansk convoys were suspended. A longer, alternative convoy route was chosen through the Suez Canal, to the Persian Gulf. Months later, as more escort vessels became available and America became a participant, the "brutal Murmansk Run" was resumed. Some losses were expected, but it was hoped that greater convoy protection would offset the gamble.

We were aware of what lay ahead of us. Slow-moving cargo ships could be extremely vulnerable. In spite of our souped-up armament and escorts, we would still be sitting ducks if we got caught. Nobody needed to urge the gunners to check their guns, or the engineers to check their engines. Nervous anticipation alone was enough to motivate everyone to make sure everything was operating smoothly and properly. The target for torpedoes was the center of a ship—the engine room and fire rooms. It was disquieting to know we were twenty feet below the waterline surrounded with high pressure steam lines. Nearby depth charging, without warning, was always unnerving. We were advised that our life expectancy was less than five minutes in the frigid Arctic waters.

Finally, the assembled ships moved out of Loch Ewe[1] and formed into convoy JW-60. There were thirty-one cargo ships, fifteen destroyers, one cruiser, two corvettes, two light British aircraft carriers and seven Russian torpedo boats protecting our convoy heading for North Russia, 1600 miles away.

Our course was set westerly into the teeth of a North Atlantic gale. A good stiff wind made our stays and guy wires sing. Rain and spray came at us horizontally. Life within the ship became treacherous. Cooking and serving food were impossible. Standing watch or keeping station was difficult. In spite of these discomforts, there was an air of optimism among all hands because these very conditions limited submarine or airplane activity. There were several sub alerts, but nothing came of them.

After two days of turbulent weather, we emerged into a more tranquil atmosphere that turned rather quickly into fog with heavy rollers. Sea conditions allowed all four lifeboats to be swung out in the ready-to-launch position, with boat covers removed. Emergency provisions in the boats and life rafts were carefully checked. We headed due north, passing Iceland. The fog persisted. It was a fine security blanket for our mission. It was not a pea soup fog that would make station-keeping difficult, but one that would hamper enemy aircraft and submarine activity. Apparently the foggy condition was a weather pattern traveling northward with us. An unexpected break in the weather suddenly

[1] Convoy JW-60 left Loch Ewe on September 15, 1944. On the same day a force of twenty-eight Lancaster bombers of RAF squadrons 9 and 617, flying from an airfield near Arkhangelsk, Northern Russia, attacked the German battleship *Tirpitz* in Norway's Altafjord. Thirteen of the bombers were armed with special "mine-bombs" and the rest attacked with 12,000-pound "Tallboy" bombs. One bombed hit the bow of the smoke-shrouded *Tirpitz*, which failed to sally out after convoy JW.60.

brought blue sky and sunshine. Our escorts became active ahead of us, and the rumble of depth charges was heard and felt. All ships went to general quarters. Distant escort activity continued for several hours. An air alert was signaled. Well astern of the convoy we saw a number of planes at two levels forming for attack. This was the classic method of pounding Russia-bound convoys: a combined sub and air assault. The air temperature dropped and immediately a beautiful and welcome fog redeveloped. Depth-charging ceased and we were once again hidden in a pervasive fog. We had lucked out, but continued working and sleeping in our life jackets. The fog fortunately continued to envelop us for several more days. It cleared as we neared the polar ice cap. Twilight lasted into late evening. It never became really dark. The northern lights were spectacular. Brilliant shafts of pink, green, blue and white danced in the sky amid undulating and pulsating, glowing, cloud-like masses moving about the heavens. We came within sight of the ice cap that fringed our northern horizon. Pack ice became a hazard.

We were well above the Arctic Circle. Over the horizon, the British battleship *Duke of York* and British cruisers *Belfast*, *Jamaica* and *Sheffield* and several more destroyers were shadowing our convoy, in case the German battleships and their cruisers decided to jump us from the Norwegian bases.

Dates and details of these times would have been totally obscured in my memory if I had not started a diary the day I arrived at Castine. Although decidedly against regulations, I maintained this daily diary which was kept in a weighted canvas pouch in my hip pocket for quick disposal. In it I recorded each day's events during all the time I was at sea.

Hitler was convinced that the Allies were planning an invasion of Norway. To counteract this imagined threat, he had moved the majority of German naval forces and substantial air elements to Norway. A number of submarines were also based there. Convoys heading to North Russia threatened German defensive strategy. The British, sensing the heavy concentration of German air and sea power in Norway, diverted thinly-stretched warships to protect the flow of materiels to the Soviets and to be alert to any sorties the Germans might launch. The Murmansk convoys became a pawn in the European conflict and were targeted for special attention. Complicating the issue was the pressure that Stalin was exerting on London and Washington to increase the flow of war supplies to North Russia, an area conceded to have among the worst weather conditions in the world.

The tough part of the trip was yet ahead. Weather conditions had blessed us so far. Our zigzag course and speed changes kept everyone on their toes. If one ship did not zig on time, or adjust to the new course quickly, it caused all other ships to act to avoid a collision. Misjudgments happened and tempers flared, but these were the only serious emergencies that troubled our voyage. Our ease of passage on this most dangerous route was remarkable.

The weather was particularly clear now. The temperatures were surprisingly mild, considering that we were skirting the ice cap. Long periods of twilight were difficult to adjust to. We were surprised to discover the effects of the Gulf Stream were found this far north. Sea birds were profuse.

We went north of Bear Island[2] and headed south into the Barents Sea, passing Spitzbergen and entered the Kola Inlet. Russian patrol craft joined our escorts. Half the convoy set course for Archangel, and we continued into Murmansk without incident. We were the first North Russian convoy to arrive unscathed.

Murmansk Harbor a wide, river bay with a plateau on either side. It is treeless, rocky and void of any visible habitation. One large pier jutted out from the only area where a few buildings and roads could be seen. Two ships were shepherded to the pier. The remainder dropped anchor to wait their turns. An old Span-

[2] Seven U-boats (U278, U-312, U-425, U-737, U-921, U-956 and U-997) of *Group Grimm* were lying in wait for convoy southwest of Bear Island. Warned by the Enigma codebreakers at Bletchley Park, the naval authorities routed JW-60 north of Bear Island.

S.S. Edward Spafford,
On the Murmansk Run, 1944

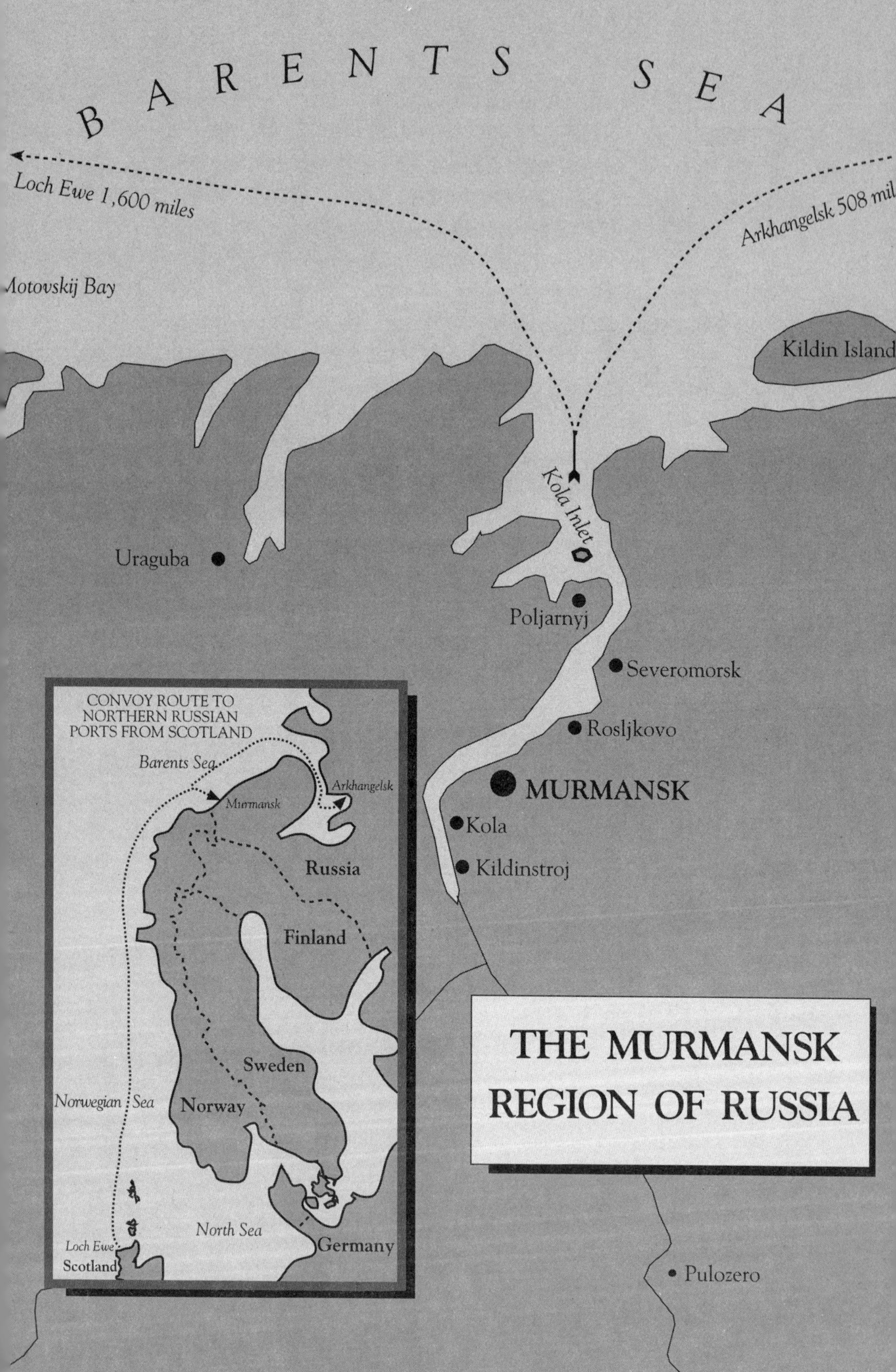

THE MURMANSK REGION OF RUSSIA

Shipyard Society

A Liberty ship and a Russian submarine in Murmansk Harbor as seen from the deck of the S.S.* Edward Spafford, *September, 1944.

ish-American War battleship which the United States had given to the Soviets was anchored at the outer harbor. It was used as a training ship, as well as an antiaircraft gunship. Another odd-looking vessel stood nearby. She was a British, heavy-lift ship with jumbo booms that handled the unloading of heavy equipment. She had been stuck in Murmansk for two years as a substitute for gantry cranes. Her British crew was berserk with boredom.

The upward bound trip to Murmansk was unexpectedly routine. Prior convoys had been savagely attacked. Air and submarine activity had taken a heavy toll of previous attempts to get war supplies through to the Soviets. Good fortune had accompanied us, first with a North Atlantic storm, followed by days of covering fog. We were fortunate, as later events would prove. Our thoughts now turned to our return trip, which could be equally hazardous.

The large number of Navy armed guard was creating friction. Added to that, the first-assistant engineer had an abrasive personality and, on various occasions, had been confrontational with just about everyone, including me. The chief mate and second mate were not on speaking terms with him. Some of the engine crew were ready to scalp him. He was argumentative and caustic with his criticism. The stage was set for morale problems and discontent. Shipboard harmony was fractured, and the anxiety of transiting a dangerous body of water kept nerves taut most of the trip.

The brand-newness of the S. S. *Edward Spafford* contributed further problems. At first, minor things such as a steam-packing gland that was not properly installed caused concern. Once at anchor in Murmansk, more serious shortcomings showed up. They continued to bedevil us the remainder of the trip.

Our first mechanical problem surfaced immediately upon leaving Portland. We began getting high-salinity content in the boiler feedwater, which could have led to serious boiler damage if unchecked. For three days we hunted for the cause, concluding that we must have a leak in the main condenser. That could mean the shutdown of the engine plant and a major repair. By chance, after a routine inspection of a feedwater tank whose purpose was filtering particles of oil from the boiler feedwater, a lunch bucket was found. Inside were two decomposed, hard-boiled eggs, an empty salt and pepper shaker and a battered thermos bottle. Our salt contamination had come from that salt shaker. Some shipyard worker had gone ashore without his lunch bucket and caused us three days of anxious searching.

We kept steam to the engine at anchorage so we could move on short notice, and stayed on sea watches. The naval gunners were on alert twenty-four hours.

At noon the following day, we moved alongside the main pier. Because of the tide fall, ships of our draft settled into the mud beside the pier at low water. Consequently, we gradually rolled to starboard five degrees as our hull settled into the river bottom.

Older Russian women filed on board and unloaded our cargo. They opened the hatches, ran our winches and did the heavy manual labor. They were all attired in similar clothing—brown quilted jackets and oversized quilted pants. Most had kerchiefs over their heads. A few had hooded coats. Nothing fazed them and they readied our railroad cranes for unloading. Chains and cables were released and swung over the side onto the pier's railroad tracks. After the engines were started, the cranes became yard switchers. Bagged grain and cases of canned food were unloaded into railcars.

So-called daylight was twilight, and twilight became darker as the sun moved south. The northern lights were a daily, vivid, spectacular sky show.

The trip into Murmansk was a revelation. It was a dismal-appearing place, made more forlorn by the lack of trees and the daily semidarkness. It reminded me of western frontier towns of the mid 1880's. There was little in Murmansk to do or to buy. It was dark and dreary most of the day. Clusters of loudspeaker horns hung from telephone poles on each street corner. Martial music and Soviet patriotic themes blared incessantly. Few people were seen.

Returning to the ship after a dull evening at the International Club, a group of us plodded along the dirt road leading to the pier and heard many voices. As we approached a rail-marshaling area, we saw a gang of middle-aged women working in the dark, replacing railroad ties and rails, with no mechanical assistance except picks, shovels and crowbars.

During the unloading process, we took on water. The hose available at the pier was very small. It took forever to top off our water tanks. This created another serious problem, but we didn't discover it until later.

When we first came alongside the pier, several Russian port officials filed on board. Among them was a doctor. I was shutting down the main engine and auxiliary machinery when summoned to the captain's cabin for a routine medical check. I made my way topside from the engine room and the purser directed me into the captain's office, where I was surprised by the doctor, a blonde, blue-eyed lady of about thirty. She proceeded to give me a thorough medical examination. I was embarrassed beyond belief.

I was still numb after I dressed and stepped into the companionway, to the smiles of several other officers. They had gathered after their exams to watch the rest of us cringe and feel stupid. The lady doctor joined us in our mess for lunch. That made it even more embarrassing. She couldn't speak English. We couldn't speak Russian. We simply ate and smiled foolishly. The Russian officials ceremoniously presented each of us with 600 rubles as a "bonus" from the Soviet government, along with a small, enameled red star as a war decoration.

We moved from the pier alongside the British heavy-lift ship where our locomotives and tanks were unloaded onto barges. From there we were shifted to the inner anchorage to wait until all cargo ships had been unloaded.

We had hardly dropped the anchor at the inner anchorage, when one of the Navy gunners mates opened the forward ammunition magazine and discovered it was flooded. This caused a major stir. It meant not only that we had depleted our ammunition by one-half, but such an occurrence required official investigations and reports.

The armed guard officer was beside himself. He was suspicious of the engineering department because we had just completed taking on water. Tempers became real hot. The ammunition magazine was drained and the compartment was entered, and it was discovered that a large, emergency, red valve had been opened and left open. Since only the armed guard crew had access to the locked ammunition magazine, the valve had to have been opened by one of them.

Then the spectre of sabotage emerged. It was considered so serious that the U. S. Naval Attache in Moscow made a special trip to Murmansk to complete an inquiry and submit a report to

Washington. There was also concern that the ammunition was unstable as a result of the flooding. The ship's crew and the armed guard were not on the best of terms and this incident only increased tension. The captain and the armed guard officer were at loggerheads the whole trip, and the flooding of the ammunition magazine intensified their cool relationship.

Just as the magazine flooding episode was resolved, the captain wanted to trim ship. This required that liquids be pumped from oil or water tanks in one location, to another location—to give the ship the desired horizontal pitch. A ship handles better if she is trimmed so the bow is a few inches higher than the stern. It was my responsibility to accomplish this routine function. I attempted to pump water from the forward tanks to the after water tanks. I discovered that no matter what I tried, I couldn't get suction on the deep tanks themselves. I was completely baffled. The only way to solve the problem was to empty the seventeen foot-high volume of water from each tank, but how? The only line coming from the tanks was apparently blocked and the blockage was at the bottom of the filled tanks.

Each liquid tank has a sounding tube that is used to measure the depth of fluid in the tank. The tube is two inches in diameter. We fabricated an inch and a half of pipe, long enough to drop down the sounding tube to the bottom of one of the deep tanks. We connected the pipe to a steam pump and began sucking water through that small-diameter pipe, knowing it would take days to empty the first of two deep tanks. It was a race against time. We had to locate the blockage and correct it before we could get underway. We certainly didn't want to miss leaving with the convoy because it meant staying in the ice-bound harbor at Murmansk until spring.

There was no way to hurry the deep-tank emptying process, so we focused on another problem that had developed. Our drinking water had a foul taste and odor, and was milky-white. We began to investigate.

There are two drinking-water tanks. We drained one, unbolted the manhole cover and went in. We found two bras, a pair of overalls, two sets of boots, three condoms, one pair of nylon panties and four lunch buckets, among other tools and incidentals. We also found that the limed-cement lining that was intended to coat the drinking-water tank was practically nonexistent. In all probability, the shipyard workers had applied it, but then had filled the tank with water before the cement had hardened. We had been drinking it, among other things, all trip. The other drinking-water tank was in worse condition. We then turned to our more serious, deep water tank problem.

The deep tank was dark and cold when emptied enough for us to enter. Armed with flashlights, we gingerly descended. As we neared bottom, we could see that there were three and a half feet of water still left in the tank. We flashed our lights around to get a general idea of the interior of the tank, and decided we had better get clothed properly and assemble the wrenches and tools we needed. An air of urgency existed because we were to be moved back to the pier for ballasting that afternoon. Ballasting meant that our departure was imminent. Resolving the water tank problem was a priority.

The chief engineer and I donned wool pants, socks and sweaters. Over these we pulled special rubberized, lifesaving suits with integral rubber boots, a rubber version of Dr. Denton's, without flap. With tools, extra flashlights and batteries, we wriggled through the manhole with some difficulty and started down into the deep tank again as the ship got underway to move to the pier. At the bottom, the remaining water level was above our waists.

We sloshed along carefully, trying to trace the suction line. The light from the flashlights barely penetrated the water. The ship in motion caused the surface of the water to surge. We used our feet to slowly follow the line, stopping at each flange to feel its condition. It was easy to trip or misstep, since hull frames and other lines crisscrossed our path. Halfway along the tank, we found our problem. A flange had a blank in it. A blank is a solid

S.S. Edward Spafford
Murmansk - 1944

circle of sheet steel that is bolted into a flange so the shipyard can pressure-test the line to check for leaks or bad connections. For some reason the shipyard workers had failed to remove the blank. This left the suction line useless. It was effectively blocked, thus preventing any flow of water.

As we pondered the problem, we heard the hull rubbing against the pier and felt the engine slow to a stop. The cold in the tank was penetrating. We had to loosen the bolts of the flange under three feet of water. We managed to get the wrench onto each bolt and with foot power, loosened them. One of us was going to get wet by leaning down to reach the bolts and remove them.

As I reached down, water ran into my rubberized suit. It was shockingly cold. I got the nuts off and handed them to the chief engineer. I pulled out the bolts to release the blank and reinserted the bolts by feeling for each hole. Since there was also a blank in the parallel starboard tank suction line, we then had to loosen a flange in that suction line so water could also be drained from that tank. With bolts finally in place and nuts twisted onto each bolt, I made for the ladder, leaving the final bolt tightening to the chief engineer.

Two steps up the ladder made me wish the rubberized suit were a Dr. Denton with flap, because I had sixty pounds of frigid water inside my suit. Each step was an effort. Each leg felt like lead and I was numb with cold. I wriggled through the manhole and simply slid onto the deck and let the trapped water gurgle out of my suit.

The water-tank suction line was fixed. We were alongside the pier and it would be hours before either of us warmed up. It had taken days to empty that tank of water. Now we had refill the tanks before leaving the pier and Murmansk. The hose the Russians provided meant a slow process was inevitable.

While we were struggling in the tank at the bottom of the ship, the Russian women built a series of wooden bins at the bottom of each hold. Made of rough-cut planks, they were eight feet deep and would receive the Russian chrome-ore ballast that was waiting on the pier to be transferred aboard us. Ballasting and taking on water continued all night.

A perfectionist by nature, our chief engineer had the look and bearing of General MacArthur. Only the corncob pipe and sun glasses were missing. A graduate of the Massachusetts Maritime Academy in the early thirties, he sailed coastwise, passenger vessels during the tough, pre-war times when ships and shipping were operated on the leanest of budgets. Low pay, poor living conditions and band-aided machinery on worn-out ships were the norm. He learned his skills well. He viewed his assignment on a Liberty ship as a step down from his steam turbine past.

Our up-and-down reciprocating engine was demeaning, yet his pride was strong enough for him to make the best of it. He had a dim view of the recent school graduates, like me, who had been pushed through classes at an accelerated pace. His disdain was apparent. I felt like a puppy dog under constant scrutiny. During my first few weeks on board, I was most uneasy and avoided him as best I could. That feeling changed as the days passed. I learned to respect his experience and he began to look at me as a student under his wing. Our relationship gradually warmed. He eased off looking over my shoulder and my confidence improved. When we headed back to the states, he had almost entirely accepted me and the engine. Strange how two people can find themselves out of step with each other, and yet, over a period of time discover mutual ground. My youth was part of the problem, combined with my fresh-out-of-school inexperience. Our age difference precluded real friendship, but we better understood each other. It was a learning experience for me and I valued my association with this authoritarian, old school chief engineer.

It was 100 days since leaving Portland. Back home, the presidential election was underway. The campaign was heated as a tired Roosevelt sought his fourth term. Although we were busy working on our engineering problems, others on the *Edward Spafford* were finding time hanging heavily. Boredom was prevalent. Bickering between the various groups on the ship became a hobby. Going ashore offered little entertainment and we were totally shut off from mail, coming or going. It had been weeks since hearing from home. The weather was raw and becoming colder as the daily twilight and darkness increased. Less time was spent on deck daydreaming, or just pacing.

Our tank troubles kept us occupied and involved, although we found time to occasionally observe the world around us. The lack of seagulls and waterfowl was noted soon after our arrival. Normally these birds flock around a ship in port, looking for garbage. Not here. There were no dogs and cats ashore. These creatures were considered as food in Murmansk. Anything that flew or walked on four legs was fair game. Food shortage was endemic in wartime Russia.

On-board pets were common on merchant ships. Several dogs and cats usually roamed the ship as mascots. They were given lots of attention and food. Pets adjusted readily to seagoing life and it was amusing to watch them adopt "sea legs" and overcome the obstructions aboard ship. They belonged to no one in particular and usually formed friendships with everyone. They became sea-smart quickly, finding some cozy cabin or space to hole-up in during inclement weather. Unfortunately, we were not alert to take precautions. All our mascots disappeared within twenty-four hours after our arrival at the dock. Apparently, they became meals for our Soviet longshore women.

The sun, low on the horizon, played games with shadows and illuminated the treeless plateau and barren hills of Murmansk. Ominous dark, snow-shower clouds created a dramatic effect as golden shafts of sunlight caressed the higher, snow-dusted points of the landscape, leaving deep shadows on the rest. It was bleak, but beautiful. The bay itself was lead-colored and cold. The clusters of ships at anchor were silhouettes swinging listlessly with the light breezes. The only sign of life was the light haze coming from the ships' smokestacks.

Snow fell daily, but usually melted soon after landing. One storm was quite heavy; its six inches of accumulation didn't melt quickly. Winter conditions were overtaking us, making our eagerness to depart more acute. Skim ice was forming along the shore.

The captain's conference was called. It lasted until late afternoon and then adjourned to a dining area, where the Soviets hosted a rather sumptuous banquet in austere surroundings. We later heard that frequent toasts were made during the meal: toasts to the British, to the Americans, the Soviets, each of the Allied leaders, the commanders in the field, and on and on. The participants were well "toasted" when they left the conference.

Four of the participants, in a "borrowed" jeep, came down the dirt road from town and, without slowing, drove onto the pier and right off the end, creating a serious reaction from all the armed sentries. The four were fished out, thoroughly chilled and slightly more sober. Other groups staggered back on foot over the next hour. A final few stragglers were herded up, put in boats and sent out to their ships. They had the balance of the night to sober up.

During the week, the Soviets mounted a major push against the Germans on the Finnish and Norwegian fronts. This heightened activity sent Soviet patrol craft, destroyers and cruisers out to sea from their naval base upriver from us. Our British escorts had arrived for our return trip and included two converted cargo vessels with aircraft and short flight decks.

Our convoy ships lit off boilers and prepared to get underway on the tide. Smoke curled from stacks, small craft shuffled around the harbor, and naval ships passed seaward in a steady stream. The harbor was a busy scene. As light snow fell, gunners were checking their weapons. Everyone, including me, was preparing for the return leg of our trip with mounting anxiety.

Ballasting continued as the trickle of water dribbled into

Murmansk,
November - 1944

our repaired deep-tanks. The ammunition from our flooded forward magazine was off-loaded since it was too unstable to keep on board. We planned to be underway on the afternoon tide.

Orders went to the fireroom to light-off number two boiler and bring it on-line by noon. The fireman on watch fired the off-line boiler, but instead of using a torch inserted into the boiler front, according to standard practice, he attempted to light-off one burner from the hot firebox brickwork. It didn't work. Rather than shutting off the oil supply to the burner, he reached for the torch, lit it and pushed it into the firebox. A muffled explosion was heard. A perfect smoke ring rolled out of the stack and continued upward, unbroken for about 300 feet. The boiler casing was blown outward on all four sides, and all of the brick baffling above the steam generating tubes fell into the firebox. A shower of puffy, black soot balls showered down onto the decks. No one was injured, but number two boiler was seriously damaged.

Quick conferences were held between the chief engineer and me and the captain and me. We could stay in Murmansk and make repairs. This would involve taking one to two days to cool down the boiler enough to get physically into the firebox and, if lucky, one day to make repairs. This choice meant that the convoy would leave without us. Within days, the harbor would ice up and we would have to spend the winter here. Our food supplies were low and there was no incoming convoy scheduled until early spring. We would not be able to leave by ourselves without escort because that would be suicide.

Our other choice was to keep both boilers on line, depart with the convoy and take our chances. If we had to shut down boiler number two, we couldn't make enough speed to stay in the convoy. That also was suicide, but it seemed our best chance. We disconnected our dockside water hose with our water tanks one-quarter full and backed out into the harbor. Other ships hauled anchor and began to move through the sub nets. Our escorts were waiting. We were homeward bound.

In our condition, several things could happen. Without baffles in place, our boiler uptake and stack temperatures could go dangerously high. The heat and fire in the boiler, instead of being baffled back and forth through the steam generating tubes, would simply go straight through and up the stack. Fuel consumption would be increased, but we had sufficient fuel on board to reach Scotland. Feedwater for number two boiler would also increase. Unfortunately, our water supply was low thanks to our tank problems. The steam from boiler number two would be abnormally super-heated. This could be a plus and give us increased engine power. Time would tell.

We maneuvered into the proper position in the convoy and began our return trip to civilization. Within a matter of hours, the paint burned off the stack uptake, and it was cherry red. The temperature gauge for the stack temperatures was off the scale. Our fuel consumption shot up and there was always the possibility that the boiler tubes would burn out under such intense heat. We carefully watched the boiler water treatment tests to prevent scale buildup within the tubes. Our first hours were anxious, watching temperature and pressure readings, checking salinity and alkalinity of the feedwater and trying to balance them. Our minds were on the machinery, not the closeness of the enemy coast.

We were being watched by German reconnaisance planes. That could mean bad news ahead. Low clouds formed in the semidarkness of the northern twilight and we relaxed from the possibility of an air attack. We were now dependent on our escorts detecting any sub activity. Our situation in the fire room appeared satisfactory. The stack and uptake temperatures were very high, but remained steady. Of greater concern was our consumption of water. With 200 people on board showering and drinking, and the galley and our boilers taking a share, our water supply was decreasing rapidly. I urged the chief engineer to advise the captain to establish water hours and water rations.

Despite our worst expectations, the run back to Scotland was devoid of serious threats. The coordinated submarine and air attacks never materialized, nor did the German surface ships attempt to sortie. The action along the Finnish-Norwegian borders apparently kept the German Air Force occupied. Our escorts kept busy screening the convoy. There were periods of intense depth-charging and sudden course changes. The British aircraft from the two escort carriers were especially active each morning and evening during twilight. They kept whatever threats that existed from materializing. Alertness was at a high pitch.

Our water supply continued to decrease rapidly. Rationing the water helped, but our consumption drew down what little we had. Number two boiler was holding its own.

Two days from Gourock, the radio announced the reelection of Franklin D. Roosevelt to a fourth term. Fighting on the continent was moving slowly, but favorably. News from the Pacific was becoming more optimistic.

Immediately after dropping anchor in Gourock, we shut down number two boiler to start the cool-down. Signals went out for the water barge and we relaxed from a tension-filled voyage while waiting to work on the cooling boiler. The skipper, gunnery officer and purser went ashore for orders and came back with the mail—the first we had received since leaving Scotland months before. I had a bunch of letters from Connie. I devoured them.

We went to work inside the boiler. It was hot and uncomfortable. About ten minutes inside was the limit before crawling out to be soaked with the water hose. Using spare baffle bricks on board with the undamaged bricks in the firebox, we rebuilt the baffles. We cleaned the water tubes and steam drums and looked for any damage. The firebox itself was carefully inspected and we found no problems.

We were slated to leave with the U. S.-bound convoy the next day. We still had not taken on water, as the water barge had not heeded our signals. The captain was extremely concerned and contacted the commodore. Late in the afternoon, the water barge finally came alongside. Our tanks were filling. We took on water all night and topped off as the ships scheduled for the homebound convoy moved out.

Number two boiler was lit and appeared to respond normally. Stack temperatures were down where they should be and our engine was warmed up and ready to go. The engine telegraph rang up "Slow ahead" and we were homeward bound. I began to consider requesting active duty in the Navy when I got home.

Thirty-three cargo ships started for North Russia, three turned back and thirty returned intact. This had never happened before. Ours was the first convoy to make this run unscathed. The only casualties were our dog and cat mascots. All our serious troubles were mechanical and urgent. People problems also created tensions. Antagonism and rivalry punctuated the voyage. The differences between the captain and the armed guard officer became so acute that the skipper had a white line painted across the bridge. He told the Navy armed guard officer in crisp four-letter words that he would shoot him if he ever crossed that white line. He meant it, too.

The British had evolved a system of arming their merchant ships with gun crews integrated into the ship's company as a department under the ship's master. They were responsible for certain ship's operations, as well as gunnery. Such a system eliminated the abrasive relationship between their ship's operating personnel and armed guard that prevailed on many of the American ships.

While in Gourock, a stores ship replenished our food needs. New ammunition also arrived for our forward magazine. About fifty of our Navy armed guard were reassigned to other ships. Fewer people on board helped lessen tension. There was less bickering and smoother relations developed. More daylight helped, also. The long periods of twilight and darkness in the Arctic hadn't improved dispositions. Now, bound for America, everyone was in a better frame of mind. It was good that this occurred. We still had trying times ahead of us.

There were fifty ships in this convoy and we had few escorts. The second day out, the radio announced the sinking of the battle cruiser *Tirpitz* by British Air Forces in a fjord in Norway. The day was stormy and this pattern continued for our homeward journey. Seasickness was prevalent. Even though ballasted, we bobbed around day and night. Few showed up for meals. Eating became a study in gymnastics. Dishes slid to the deck. Glasses spilled. Silverware gyrated around the table. When eating, we held one hand on to the table and tried to eat with the other. Sleeping was also hazardous. Violent pitching and rolling required a spread-eagle position to prevent landing on deck. Books, typewriters and loose gear became missiles. Taking a shower required dexterity. Soap on a rope was a must.

I found stormy conditions fascinating. The magnitude of the ocean and the force of storms were compelling to observe. I spent hours watching mountainous waves through the wheelhouse porthole, or standing on the lee side of the boat deck, observing the other ships in convoy slamming into waves. Even under the worst conditions, crazy little seabirds darted above the crests.

Engine room watches during rough weather were particularly tedious on a Liberty ship. It was necessary to manually control the reciprocating engine, due to the propeller coming out of the water as the ship bucked the seas. Standing four hours at the throttle, attempting to judge the moment the propeller emerged from the water, was demanding and tiring. If the propeller were not throttled, the R.P.M.'s increased rapidly and violently shook the whole ship. It was possible to snap the propeller shaft or lose the propeller.

Standing a throttle watch meant hanging on to piping with your left arm and working the throttle continuously with your right arm. It meant staying alert and trying to guess the pitching motion of the ship. Maintaining the proper water levels in the boilers was equally demanding for the fireman on watch. The engine and fire room deck plates were oily and very slippery. One could misjudge the motion of the ship easily and find himself, as if on rollerskates, heading for a bad tumble. Movable objects were tied down securely. However, as the seas became rougher and the ship responded with deeper rolls and harder pitching, tools, oil drums and grease cans sometimes broke loose and created a sudden and serious danger.

Muscles ached trying to compensate for the ship's tossing about. Bruises were common from banging into hatchways and bumping against bulkheads. I managed to sleep. I managed to eat. I managed to exist in this topsy-turvy environment. Most others didn't fare as well. Socializing and entertainment ceased. Day after day of rough weather seemed endless. The only compensation was the constant thought that we were heading home.

The danger of enemy action was greatly lessened by the turbulent sea. If conditions were bad on our ship, the naval escorts must have had deplorable living conditions, since they were smaller, lighter vessels. The North Atlantic was a violent master.

The seas moderated somewhat on Thanksgiving Day. Sunrise heralded a clear sky. The cooks reorganized the galley. By noontime they had prepared a Thanksgiving dinner with most of the fixin's. About half the hands turned out to sample it. The third engineer, third mate and all three radio operators were bedridden with seasickness. The skipper and chief engineer were up and about, but declined to eat.

During the day, we passed out of the Gulf Stream and observed a twenty degree drop in the seawater temperatures. The clouds thickened. The wind increased and we were back into stormy conditions, heavy seas and throttle watches again.

A signal from the commodore informed us that the *Edward Spafford* was scheduled to be routed to Portland, Maine. I thanked my lucky stars to be on the only ship in the convoy chosen to head for Portland, and I was the only person on board who was from Maine! I was on throttle watch when they called from the bridge to give me the news. My spirits soared. Golly, did they soar!

The storm worsened. The ship was rolling violently. Five ships fell astern of the convoy during the night with mechanical troubles. At dawn, the escorts were depth-charging ahead of our track. We were 300 miles off Nova Scotia and had eight hours of dull sunshine and easing turbulence.

I had started packing my bags, preparing to leave the ship. I kept thinking how surprised Connie would be since she had not heard from me in months.

Inclement weather persisted. We were well off Cape Cod and the commodore had not released us and we were still heading south. I became concerned. My hopes were fading. The radio alerted us that a late-season tropical storm was moving up the Carolina coast and our convoy was being rerouted to avoid its track. As we changed course, so did the tropical storm that intensified into a hurricane. After an especially stormy North Atlantic crossing, we were plunging headlong into a dangerous Atlantic hurricane.

All our lifeboats and life rafts were torn overboard; potato lockers, stanchions and ladders were ripped loose. Watertight doors and hatches were bashed in and the deckhouse quarters were aslosh with water. Ventilators were twisted and leaking. Water was running into the engine room. The convoy scattered with ships in all conditions of breakdown. Propellers were lost. Steering engines were jammed and electrical circuits shorted out.

Our greatest danger was from the collapsing ballast-shoring bins in our holds. Boards and trusses gave way under the violent pitching and rolling. The chrome-ore ballast had shifted and spilled out, causing a permanent list to port. Both fuel and water were pumped to different tanks in an attempt to compensate for the list. The captain ordered all personnel not standing watch, into the holds to shovel the loose ore and to reinforce the remaining shoring boards and supports. Six hours of physical effort accomplished little. Each roll and pitch nullified the efforts.

The galley-stove burner panel was smashed. The galley itself was a shambles. Broken dishes, pots and pans, glasses, assorted spices, flour, ketchup, vinegar and molasses sloshed back and forth in a foot of seawater. Toilets and companionways were flooded. Antennas sheared off, but the ship was intact and still under power. The *Spafford* was one of only a few ships in the convoy that came out of the hurricane under her own power. Others were disabled and several were in distress. Urgent radio traffic filled the airwaves. Tugs from New York, Baltimore and Philadelphia were busy the next few days towing damaged ships into port. All of this distress was censored for home consumption.

I managed to be in the wheelhouse during the peak of the hurricane, watching the drama of nature. Seas were estimated to be fifty to sixty feet. The crests of waves, mixed with the rain, were blowing horizontally in sheets. I watched other ships plummet over the crests with propellers spinning wildly, then totally disappear. With each plunge, our ship shuddered and shook.

You could feel the vibration of the engine racing throughout the ship when the propeller left the water. The main seawater intake, located in the center of the ship's bottom, was sucking air as the hull pitched over the cresting waves. This caused the condenser vacuum to drop and the engine to slow without warning, at a moment when engine power was essential to keep us from broaching sideways to the wind and waves. Without warning, it became relatively calm with dull sunshine and was oppressively humid and warm. The roar of the storm was replaced with an unearthly quiet. We were in the very eye of the hurricane. Several other ships were still with us in this strange environment. Ahead of us, we could see a wall of water.

Again we plunged into very rough seas and strong hurricane winds, but it moderated noticeably in a short time and within hours returned to nearly normal conditions. Damage was assessed and we reversed course to steam to Portland independently. The

sun broke through and by sundown the weather and the sea were subdued. It was strange not to see any other ships around us. I didn't sleep at all that night with the excitement of arriving in Portland. We were still listing noticeably to port.

We entered Portland Harbor at 10 o'clock the following night. I stood anxiously on the bridge as the Portland lightship came into view. I watched Cape Elizabeth's familiar landmarks as we picked up our pilot. We dropped anchor close by Fort Allen Park at the Eastern Promenade. I was too excited to sleep. I paced the deck all night.

The next morning, Sunday, December 3, 1944, we passed through the South Portland bridge to the coal pier in Pleasantdale, South Portland. I waited impatiently for the ship to tie up and put the gangway over. Customs, immigration and port officials came on board. I was allowed to go ashore to make a phone call. I called my folks. They had not heard from me for months and were greatly surprised to learn I was in South Portland. They said Connie was on duty until noon and that they would be right over to pick me up. We parked in front of the nurses' home to wait for Connie. She and two classmates walked from duty at the hospital to the nurses' residence. The look on her face when she saw me was worth the months we had been apart. She quickly changed and we went home for a marvelous Sunday dinner. I quietly celebrated my two years at sea.

Left:** The S.S.* Jeremiah O'Brien, ***one of two Liberty ships afloat, steams toward Portland Head Light, Cape Elizabeth, Maine, as it makes its way into Portland Harbor in August of 1994. The** O'Brien **stopped in Portland en route to its home port of San Francisco following a visit to the D-Day invasion beaches of France's Normandy coast. *Don Johnson photo*

Chapter Four

Buzz Bombs, Fog & Tankers

I was one of the lucky ones to spend Christmas of 1944 at home. I made the best of it and enjoyed every minute, spending as much time with Connie as her time off allowed. I had been away a long time and being home again was a great feeling!

I learned after my first trip that people at home weren't really interested in hearing about my experiences. I was bursting to talk about what I had seen and done. I soon recognized that I was talking to deaf ears. It was not that they didn't want to listen. It was because they couldn't comprehend or understand.

Mountainous seas and blocks of gutted buildings and days of anguish were beyond their ability to grasp. The nights of depth-charging and tedious, tension-filled watches could not be imagined. I discovered that questions like, "Did you see much action?" should be answered with a simple "Yes" or "No," and to let it go at that. Or, "Was it a rough trip?" "It sure was." No further elaboration was wanted, or needed. It was wartime and few really desired to hear the details.

While on leave, I went to the First Naval District in Boston to request active Navy duty. I was interviewed by the assignment officer. He listened to my request, looked at my written application and smiled. Then he told me why he couldn't approve. He confided that there were eight ships in Boston Harbor at that moment that were prevented from joining a convoy because of the shortage of licensed engineering officers to operate them. It was therefore impossible for him to approve my request under such circumstances, since I was needed on merchant ships. Engineers were in particularly short supply at that time. I returned home disappointed.

Portland was overrun with sailors and shipyard workers. War fever and the disruption of normalcy changed the lives of most. The struggle in the Pacific and in Europe brought solemn casualty figures to the home front. A wide spread attitude of "live for today" was apparent. Who could predict what tomorrow might bring?

Housewives, restaurants and institutions were struggling to prepare innovative foods in spite of shortages. Gasoline rationing allowed twenty-five gallons per month, enough fuel for about 300 miles. Meat and sugar were among the hundreds of items strictly rationed. Cigarettes, candy, nylons and Scotch Whiskey were prime items on the black market. Every individual was participating in the war effort in one way or another. People not directly employed in the war effort volunteered their time as air raid wardens, backup fire fighters, hospital assistants and U.S.O. participants. Never had our country been so totally mobilized, or as completely unified in a single cause. Optimism in the outcome of the war was strong.

Planning ahead was stifled by the uncertainty of today and tomorrow. Resiliency became the necessity of life. Change became normal. Friendships were brief and transient. School friends and relatives were scattered afar. Daily living was disrupted throughout society.

All of Portland and other east coast cities were blacked out at night. Sixteen-inch coastal defense batteries lined the Casco Bay islands and Cape Elizabeth's shore. An elaborate underground command and control center located near Two Lights linked east coast defenses. Portland, like most American cities, was a beehive of wartime activity.

Connie was determined to complete her nurses' training. Marriage meant giving up what she had set out to do and she felt she would always regret quitting. The risk of eloping was too great to chance. The only course open to us was to gain official permission from the superintendent of nurses. Thus, each time I came home from a voyage, we called for an appointment with the superintendent of nurses. Each time she was very gracious and almost sympathetic, but the answer was no. We met with her on five occasions. Once we took Connie's mother with us for reinforcement, but each time the answer was negative. It seemed hopeless.

I went back to sea, dejected and disappointed. Doubts were uneasy thoughts to live with. The uncertainty of the times simply magnified my ability to rationalize our situation. Her first letters began arriving at the next port and my doubts would once again be controllable—her expressions were reassuring. I felt better. My longing increased and, when I got back to Portland after each trip, my determination to convince her to get married was at a high pitch again. Long, heated discussions only brought us back to square one. It was an endless circle.

On January 13, 1945, I received my booster shots for typhus, tetanus and small pox. The next morning I signed on the S. S. *William Dobson*, a new Liberty ship that had almost completed loading at Pier 1 in Portland. With very sore arms, I lugged my seabag and suitcase through an empty, snow covered field and long pier to board the ship. I was very down in the dumps. I said goodbye to Connie that morning, as she went back to duty.

The *Dobson* was taking on water and fuel. Shipyard workers were still on board, finishing painting and other last-minute jobs. Carpenters were busy building wooden cases over the deck cargo, which consisted of crated aircraft and aircraft engines. The main deck was completely filled with cargo, wire-cabled to the deck. A catwalk was built over the tops of the crates. I had never seen a Liberty so heavily loaded. Standing on the main deck, it seemed I could almost touch the water's surface.

Once settled in my cabin, I met the other officers. I was pleasantly surprised. They were the youngest group with whom I had ever sailed. The chief engineer and skipper were in their late twenties. The other mates and engineers were all under thirty-five. I was immediately impressed with the cheerfulness and, friendly attitude of this group. It was a good beginning. I learned that the majority of the crew were southerners. For some reason, I was destined to sail with southern sailors and learn to like southern ways of cooking.

The effect of my booster shots left me with a mild headache and fever. Sea watches began at noon and, as second engineer, I went below at noon to begin my first watch. My watch partners were also refreshingly young. Both boilers were on line and the engine was at standby. At one p.m., we got underway.

After passing through the South Portland bridge, we spent three hours off Fort Allen Park, swinging ship to calibrate and check the navigation instruments. At dusk, we headed out the channel with shipyard workers and carpenters still hard at work. When the pilot boat came alongside, they left and we headed for New York via the Cape Cod Canal.

We dropped anchor for the night in Smithtown Bay, Long Island. The next morning we moved down Long Island Sound to City Island where the captain and gunnery officer attended the convoy conference. Once again underway, we passed through Hell's Gate, down the East River to Staten Island and anchored for a short period. The captain and gunnery officer arrived from

Joining the S.S. William Dobson
Portland, Maine
January - 1945

the convoy conference and we got underway again through Ambrose Channel. During the night, we formed into a convoy and headed in a northeasterly direction.

We enjoyed two days of nice smooth weather. The machinery was behaving well and I became further acquainted with the people with whom I would be spending the next months. I liked them. It was a completely new attitude and spirit than my previous trips. They were friendly and professional. Although the war was still serious, the conditions in the Atlantic were more under control. The new snorkel submarines were being deployed by the enemy and these caused a new challenge. However, more and better escorting countered the danger. Shipboard life was more relaxed.

The S. S. *William Dobson* was heavily loaded and plunged through the sea, hardly rolling or pitching. Waves surged over the bow, breaking on the main deck which was awash most of the time. Some of the deck cargo shifted and was damaged. Wire cables holding down the cargo snapped and twisted. The wooden catwalk to the forward gun tubs was knocked askew. Seawater had penetrated the deckhouse companionways through a damaged hatch and sloshed around. The days and nights generally became more pleasant for the wintertime North Atlantic. Several depth-charging incidents, well ahead of us, reminded us there was still a war going on and yet the trip was more like a cruise with a cordial group of tourists. As we neared the United Kingdom, a light fog enveloped us and the sea became pleasantly tranquil. It gave us a good opportunity to watch the porpoise, whales and sea birds. Our eastbound trip was uneventful. The return trip would not be so peaceful.

The color of the ocean changed from azure blue to green as we neared land. The convoy pattern was changed as we traversed the Irish Sea and eventually dropped anchor off the White Cliffs of Dover. The following morning, with pilot aboard we proceeded to the Thames and into London. We tied up at a grain pier and the unloading began. German V-1 buzz bombs were still being launched toward England and the new V-2 rockets were confounding the experts.

Those of us not on watch were on deck as we steamed up the Thames towards London. For us, it was a sightseeing trip. We were attracted by several contrails high in the sky; trailing graceful plumes, curving and crisscrossing one another. Suddenly a flash blossomed, followed by the sound of a distant explosion. We had witnessed the downing of a buzz bomb by high-flying fighter planes.

The approach of lower-flying buzz bombs was usually seen and heard. You were prepared for its impact. The newer V-2 rockets provided no warning, whatever. They were frightening. This new weapon had a fearful effect on all who were within its range.

A large number of the buzz bombs were coaxed beyond populated London by ingenius British deception. The new V-2's were not as easily diverted. They were less accurate and more destructive.

We were just sitting down for lunch when there was a tremendous explosion, followed by a sound like hail on a tin roof. All sixteen of us jumped up and shot for the door. A V-2 rocket had impacted on a barge in the dock area. It caused no major damage or serious injuries. Shrapnel and pieces of metal landed on our deck and were imbedded in our shrapnel shield protecting the pilothouse.

Thinking back after this happened, I realized a strange reaction had occurred. Fifteen people had all jammed into one doorway trying to exit. I was the only one to head for the other doorway. I have wondered about my individual reaction many times since.

Another close encounter happened when we were ashore

Saturday, February 10, 1945
41st Day—324 Days to Follow

CAME BACK AT 8^00 THIS MORNING WITH PURSER. PUMPED OIL TO BARGE MOST ALL DAY. WAS GOING TO SHOW WITH FIRST TONIGHT BUT SNOW, AND SLEET STOPPED US. TO BED EARLY. PLAN TO GO TO WESTMINSTER ABBEY IN THE MORNING, WITH SECOND MATE. HAVE TRIED TO CONTANT JIN BURNAHAM WHO IS SUPPOSED TO BE AT ONE OF THESE HOSPITALS —

Sunday, February 11, 1945
42nd Day—323 Days to Follow

VERY EXCITING BUT WET DAY. WENT UPTOWN WITH 2ND MATE. HIRED GUIDE, AND VISITED BUCKINGHAM, ST. JAMES PALACE, GEORGE VI PALACE, ADMIRALTY 10 DOWNING ST, HOUSE OF LORDS AT COMMONS, THE TOWER OF LONDON, MADAME TOUSARDS, AND WENT TO SERVICES AT WESTMINSTER ABBEY. BACK BEFORE DARK, WET, AND TIRED

Monday, February 12, 1945
43rd Day—322 Days to Follow

HOLIDAY TODAY. HAD THE WATCH FROM 5 LAST NIGHT, TO 5 TONITE. 1ST ASSISTANT, PURSER, 2ND MATE, AND MYSELF WENT UPTOWN TONITE TO SEE "THE THIN MAN COMES HOME" WHICH I HAD ALREADY SEEN. CAME RIGHT BACK FOLLOWING SHOW. FINISHED UNLOADING YESTERDAY AND SHIFTED SHIP LAST NIGHT TO BALLASTING DOCK. EXPECT TO LEAVE WEDNESDAY NOON. HAVE HAD A GOOD TIME HERE, AND HAS BEEN MY BEST TRIP. UNDECIDED ABOUT STAYING. WAR LOOKS AS THOUGH IT MIGHT BE TERMINATING SOON. RUSSIANS ARE MAKING MARVELOUS HEADWAY. BUZZ BOMB LANDED TOO CLOSE LAST NIGHT, BEING A SHORT DISTANCE AWAY. THEY CONTINUE TO LAND DAILY, SOME QUITE CLOSE ———

Two pages from the author's diary written when he was in London during the buzz bomb attacks.

in the vicinity of Picadilly. A loud nearby explosion startled us. We went in the direction of the explosion two blocks away. A V-2 rocket had come down on a busy street close to a subway entrance. Casualties were many and carnage was all too visible. We arrived at the same time as the fire and police. Ambulances were screaming from all directions. It was a terrible sight. The buildings facing the street were opened up like eggshells. Casualties were all over the area. A large crater indicated the point of impact. Many bodies were scattered around the subway entrance.

Soon after our ship arrived in the East India dock area, mail was brought on board. Many letters from Connie and my family arrived and an envelope from Washington, D. C. Prior to this trip, I sat for my first engineer's license, a tedious five-day, eight-hour-a-day exam. As the yeoman typed my papers, he realized that I was not yet twenty-one years of age, as required under federal law. A hurried consultation and a long distance call to the Coast Guard commandant in Washington resulted in my receiving an official letter stating that I had passed the exam, but lacked the required age for being issued the license. It would be sent to me on my birthdate four months hence. My delayed license was in the envelope with a note stating I was the youngest person to pass the first engineer's examination up to that time.

While we were in London, survivors of a Liberty ship that had been sunk just outside the mine field leading into the Thames were landed. That gave us food for thought. We were jolted by two rocket bombs that struck not too far away. One landed in an area already leveled by German bombers. The other hit a nearby warehouse area and created a formidable fire, but fortunately there were few casualties. The day we were ballasting, prior to leaving, one buzz bomb leveled a church on the other side of the dock area.

We left on Valentine's Day, 1945, as several rocket bombs impacted on East London. We anchored outside the sub nets. We heard that several coastal ships had been sunk the previous day in the Straits of Dover. After a day of thick fog, we formed into a sixty-six ship, westbound convoy. We were alerted that U-boats were active in the area.

We passed the hulk of a ship sunk two days earlier. Only the tops of her deckhouse and masts were visible. The convoy was strung out two ships abreast and thirty-three long. The anti-submarine activity was intense all day and into the night. Two ships leading the convoy were torpedoed. One was sunk. We sailed right through the floating debris as patrol craft were picking up survivors. Depth-charging was very near and almost continuous. British aircraft were with us all the time. Course and speed changes were endless. Escorts charged right through our columns, dropping depth charges. Each explosion lifted our ship with a solid jolt. It was the most intensive depth-charging I had ever experienced.

Eighteen hours of the most concentrated action had kept us anxious and on edge. Once into the Irish Sea, the convoy re-formed into an eight-column spread of ships. That night we penetrated a fog that kept us equally tense for the next four days.

Although our ships were separated by only five to six hundred feet, the fog was so dense that we didn't see another ship for four days. Station-keeping in the convoy was controlled by periodically sounding each ship's whistle with its numerical position in the convoy. For example, one short blast, followed by three, indicated ship number one in the third column. This resulted in a twenty-four hour orchestration of ships' whistles. Sleeping was quite difficult, even for me.

The tension of staring into thick fog with invisible ships close beside, ahead and astern, made watch-standing on the bridge a test of nerves. Equally difficult was the engine room watch because of continous engine speed changes to prevent overtaking the ships ahead, or dropping back on the ships astern. Watch-standers came off duty completely drained. After three days of thick unending fog I dallied on the boat deck when I was relieved from my engine watch. I was daydreaming, staring into the fog from the starboard side, listening to the various whistle signals, when a most eerie event happened right before my eyes. It was a frightening few moments.

The bow of a ship appeared dimly—like an apparition—from the dense fog and aimed straight at us. I was powerless to act since I was too far from the bridge to warn them. I watched with growing apprehension as the ship became more visible and continued advancing directly at us. I could see the bow lookout. I watched him grab his phone and I actually heard him call to his bridge.

Simultaneously, I heard our engine room telegraph ring and felt the vibration of our engine responding. I watched as our two vessels slowly turned onto parallel courses, closing one another within a few feet, so close I could reach out and almost touch the other ship. The distance gradually increased and she slipped back into the fog without a trace. I hardly breathed as I watched the event. It was a chilling moment. The hair on my neck was still tense.

Throughout the convoy, similar close shaves happened. Minor collisions sheared off lifeboats and rafts, bent stanchions and dished hull plating. By some miracle, all sixty-six ships survived the four days of sailing blind. Two days of intense anti-sub activity, plus the four days of fog, had left everybody tired and done in. We emerged into a calm sea and warm, sunny day. It was almost as if we were being rewarded for our ordeal. Relaxation became the rule.

The *Dobson* was a happy ship. The younger group worked well together. It was a spirited and cheerful relationship; abrasive situations never got out of hand. There was more sociability, lingering over meals and less antipathy between departments. She was a ship that ran smoothly. It was evident in many ways. The engine spaces were neat and clean. The deck spaces were kept painted and tidy. No one begrudged a little extra effort to put things away or to fix up what was obvious. Even the skipper and armed guard officer got along amicably, which was remarkable. We all had more in common and we got on well together.

Thoughts of Portland began crowding in as we got closer to the east coast. Letters were reread for any hint of a change of Connie's viewpoint. A longing for a stronger decision haunted me.

The weather continued fair and the ocean was unusually calm for several days. Night presented a splendorous display of stars. Visibility was superb and all the ships in the convoy could be clearly seen. The escort carriers and the destroyer screen had little activity and probably enjoyed the weather as much as we. Four-engine patrol aircraft were now within range and covering our advance. The days moved along peacefully. It was not to last. During the fourth night, the seas began to build up and, toward morning, we were into a first-class storm.

Throttle watches and violent pitching and rolling bounced us around for the next twenty-four hours. A number of the ships had breakdowns. When the storm abated, there were only forty-one ships still in ragged formation. The others were either waiting for tows or struggling independently to port. We and one other Liberty were signaled to proceed to Baltimore. We peeled off and cranked the engine up to 7600 RPM's and raced for the Chesapeake. We anchored off Cape Henry for the night. The next morning, with pilot on board, we arrived in Baltimore.

I made plans to head home after my payoff. The chief engineer asked me to make another trip as first-assistant engineer on the *Dobson*. I agreed, providing I could dash home. Just before my arrival in Portland, my father received a call from the chief engineer saying that the *Dobson* was being sent to another port the next day and to return at once. I called Northeast Airlines at the Portland Airport to make a reservation for the seven a.m. New York flight. I was told that the airports in Boston and Portland were closed because of a winter storm. There was no hope except to catch the eight a.m. train to Boston the next morning and make plane connections from there. For all my effort I never got together with Connie.

I was ticketed on a Boston-New York flight which was delayed while the runways at Logan Airport were cleared. Arriving at 4:30 p.m. in Baltimore, I hailed a taxi and sped to the waterfront. I made it to the pier just in time to see the S. S. *William Dobson* disappear down the bay into fog. I had a desperate feeling as the impact of my situation sunk in. What to do? Where to go? I was exhausted and hungry. All my clothes and gear were on the *Dobson*. A sinking feeling gripped me.

I went to the War Shipping office and explained my plight. They would not tell me much except that it would be smart if I went to New Orleans. I teamed up with another engineer and we booked a compartment on a New Orleans-bound train. That didn't leave me much money. It was a long, slow trip. On the second day, my friend met an Army nurse and they spent most of the day together in the parlor car. That night, he didn't return to our compartment. I never saw him again. During the night, the last five Pullman cars were detached and hooked to a California-bound train. All his personal goods, clothing and baggage were still in our compartment.

When I arrived at the War Shipping office in New Orleans, I was told that the *Dobson* was due in port in two days. I checked into the Roosevelt Hotel with a second mate awaiting another ship to share expenses. On the second morning, he and his baggage were gone and I was stuck with his bill. This left me almost penniless.

I finally boarded the *Dobson* and within five hours we were underway, destined for Houston, Texas. I learned that the chief engineer and captain had held the ship in Baltimore as long as they could, waiting for me. Then they had to get underway. A new first-assistant engineer had been rushed on board to take my place. They expected to see me at the pilot station at Norfolk, but heavy fog prevented their stopping to drop off the pilot. If I wanted to make the next trip on the *Dobson*, it would have to be as second engineer rather than as first engineer. My response required little thinking. I liked the ship and the people on it and signed on without hesitancy.

We were ten days loading grain and mixed cargo in Houston. The shift from munitions and war equipment reflected the way the European conflict was going. It was an enjoyable ten days with little on-board work to accomplish.

After loading, the *Dobson* returned down the Houston ship canal, a forty-mile waterway that goes through several Texas suburbs and the Texas countryside. We passed through the Gulf, around the Florida Keys and slid past Miami at night, staying close to the coast before dropping anchor off Virginia Beach. The news from Europe was most favorable and the war there seemed to be near an end. At 4:10 p.m., the first announcement of President Roosevelt's death was broadcast. It shocked everybody.

A day and a half later, we formed into a convoy, heading for the Mediterranean. The first night out, there was a substantial amount of anti-submarine activity. Depth charging and snowflake illumination lasted for hours. The U-boats apparently didn't know the war was hopeless for them.

A week of superb weather made this period a delightful stretch. I placed a canvas cot on the wing of the bridge and slept there at night. The moon and the stars were sharp and beautiful. The swish and splash of the ship plowing through the water was like music. Sleep came easily.

On the ninth day out, I developed a fever. I came off watch from the engine room at four a.m., aching all over. When I was awakened for breakfast, I was covered with red blotches of hives and my temperature was elevated. My feet and hands were swollen and I had a severe headache. The purser, who also acted as medical first aid person, became concerned and signaled the doctor on the convoy commodore's ship. His response came back to treat me for rheumatic fever and take me off the watch list. I was to stay in bed and take four aspirin every two hours, twenty-four hours a day. The chief engineer began standing my watch and the steward served my meals in the cabin. I became a passenger.

The hives worsened. My joints ached and I couldn't shake the headache, in spite of the heavy dose of aspirin. I began to feel slightly better the day we passed through Gibraltar. I spent most of the day on a cot on the boat deck as a sightseer. Some different from the first time I went through Gibraltar, I thought. My mind was dwelling instead on the implications of having rheumatic fever and how that might affect my life. Two days later, we docked in Algiers.

The day that Adolf Hitler's suicide became worldwide headlines, the purser took me to a British field hospital twenty miles inland over bumpy roads. A British major checked me and took blood. My heart appeared to be okay, but I had a low-grade temperature and my blood sedimentation rate suggested rheumatic fever. The hives had lessened, but were still bothersome. The major wanted to keep me there for six weeks for treatment. Both the purser and I put up such resistance that he relented and allowed me to return to the ship, but made us take a letter to our captain urging that I be kept immobilized. Luckily, the skipper thought it best for me to remain on board so that I could be treated on our return to the States. A portion of our cargo had been unloaded and we were directed to move down the coast to Bizerte the next morning.

Bizerte was in shambles. The harbor was devastasted with sunken ships scuttled across the channel. Military engineers had cut the sunken hulls in two, allowing passage right through them. Buildings were gutted and the waterfront was flattened. We tied up to the quay and unloading began.

That afternoon, the purser took me three miles inland to an American military hospital for more blood testing and examination. The doctor there was not convinced that I had rheumatic fever and approved my standing watch once again, but noted I was to be kept on light work duties. I still had pain in my joints and my hands and feet tended to swell after five or six hours. My temperature was back to normal, the hives had gone and I was somewhat relaxed.

Upon my return to the ship, news of the end of the war in Europe had just been broadcast. All work and activity stopped. As darkness fell, a spontaneous celebration of V.E. Day commenced. The antiaircraft guns on several ships began firing skyward. Soon all ships joined in. Machine guns, Very flare guns and even hand guns were firing into the sunset. Tracer bullets and flares lit the sky. On shore, British and American Army people joined in. Local Arabs were storming around on horseback, firing their rifles. The next morning, my temperature was elevated again. I had a splitting headache and swollen hands and feet. I remained in bed the next four days with meals again being delivered to my cabin.

After six days of unloading in Bizerte, we were sent to Tunis for final unloading and then we steamed back to Oran. I remained a semi-invalid passenger. I was taken ashore to the U. S. Army dispensary for further tests and examinations. The doctors there advised me to stay with the ship so that I could be checked into a hospital on our return to the states. A letter to the skipper suggested no watch standing or other duties. Five days later we set sail with thirty-eight other ships for America. The chief engineer stood my watches and I felt worse than ever.

Halfway across the Atlantic we were instructed to turn on our lights and proceed independently to New Orleans. The convoy disbanded, each ship heading off on a different course. At sundown, blackout ports were removed, navigation lights were turned on and we moved independently at top speed. It was a strange feeling to walk about the ship now fully-illuminated and to be by ourselves after so many months of blackouts and convoys. After such a long period of tension from depth charging and being constantly alert, a sense of relief and relaxation settled over the ship. Our armed guard crew and armament were now completely obsolete.

Days before when we docked in Bizerte, the pilot miscalculated our speed and angle. Our propeller struck the concrete pier and we couldn't assess the damage. We felt a slight vibration at certain speeds, so we realized some damage had been done. When the convoy was disbanded we cranked up to speed, our first twenty-four hours averaged over twelve knots with a distinct vibration. Whacking the concrete pier had apparently increased the pitch of our prop. The vibration kept us alert watching the shaft bearings for build-up from friction.

Shortly after being directed to proceed independently, a spontaneous suggestion stimulated everyone. Let's fix the ship up. The idea took hold. Paint brushes began flying. The engine and fire rooms were further cleaned up and painted. Brass was polished and deck plates wire-brushed until they sparkled. Even the rag and refuse cans were repainted. A similar effort was occurring on deck. Everyone pitched in enthusiastically, with the skipper, chief engineer and gunnery officer wielding paint brushes. I sketched out an idea to repaint the hull in two shades of gray to create a streamline effect like a Greyhound bus. My idea was adopted and repainting began immediately.

Even though I was still achy and swollen, I managed to get up on a bosun's chair at the stack and, with crayon, outlined the form of a Bugs Bunny lying in a relaxed position with one arm propping up his head and the other holding a bottle of beer. The other guys loved it. There were six of them painting, under my direction. Bugs Bunny filled both sides of the stack. We were just about to paint in the label of a New Orleans beer, when a signal changed our destination to Houston. The guys went to work painting a Houston beer label instead. Peace caused us to redirect our energies.

Never was another Liberty ship cleaned up and fancied up as the S. S. *William Dobson*. Weather conditions were ideal for this frenzied, all-hands effort. Those not standing watch were eagerly volunteering their two cents worth. I became the unofficial director-producer of the effort, in spite of my limited physical contribution.

We passed through the "Hole in the Wall" in the Bahamas and the next day came within sight of Florida. We attracted airplanes, both civil and military, which made low passes over us since they couldn't believe our appearance. They had seen plain gray ships for several years and our jaunty look caught them by surprise. Passing along the coast, ships gave us blasts of their horns. This kind of recognition simply drove our crew and officers to clean even better and to paint more carefully. Inside and outside, we really sparkled. Passing up the Houston Ship Canal earned us all kinds of waves and horn tooting. When we tied up

S.S. William Dobson
May - 1945

at the dock in Houston, waiting at the gangway was a Jax beer truck with ten cases of complimentary beer for the crew of the *Dobson*. A truck loaded with gold bars would not have been received with more enthusiasm.

The S. S. *William Dobson*, built in South Portland, was a very special ship. She was truly one of a kind in both spirit and looks.

I was transported to the Public Health Hospital in Houston for another round of examinations. I had to return each day for further tests and get the results of the previous probings. I urged from the onset that I be allowed to return to Portland to my own family physician for treatment. The public health doctors diagnosed my problem as a collagen disease, not rheumatic fever. Collagen disease starts when an allergy triggers an auto-immune response in the body—sort of a body defense system fighting itself. In the end, they did agree to my returning home and issued a thirty-day medical leave-renewable certificate. I was very pleased.

With all goodbyes said and bags packed, I left the guys on the *Dobson* and boarded a two-engine Lockheed for a non-stop night flight to New York. Passenger capacity was around thirty people with a single row of seats on either side of the center aisle. I had been feeling good during the previous few days except for mild aches, low temperature and swelling hands and feet. I relaxed as we took off into an overcast night. It was great to be back in the states heading north.

The cabin lights had been dimmed as most passengers were trying to sleep. A few were reading. The flight was relatively smooth with a few dips. I was reminded of Connie's flight from Portland to Bangor to attend my graduation months before at Castine. Her flight was very bumpy and rough. I had arranged for a taxi to meet her at the airport and take her to the academy at Castine. It had been a rough bumpy trip also. She arrived after the graduation ceremony had begun and quickly located my folks and joined them. Unbeknown to either Connie or my folks and a total surprise to me, ten of us were to graduate with honors. That moment our names were read and we proceeded to the stage was among the proudest of my life. I looked at Connie and my folks and felt a satisfaction seldom experienced before. In my wildest imagination, I never expected to graduate with honors. Just thinking about it after all this time made me very emotional.

Suddenly, my reverie was broken by a burst of light outside my window followed by a second flash of fire. The cabin lights were turned on and the stewardess sprang into action. I could see the engine propeller on my side being feathered, as intermittent streaks of flame illuminated passengers. The plane was yawing, as the pilot attempted to control the flight. He informed us by intercom that one engine had caught fire but we were not in real danger. He assured us the aircraft was airworthy on one engine.

Tallahassee Airport was notified of our emergency and we received clearance to land there. Within a short time, we saw city lights all around as we broke out of the clouds and made a smooth landing. Fire trucks and ambulances surrounded us. Busses ferried us to the terminal. The flight terminated there.

A hasty check at the various airlines confirmed that all New York flights were booked for the next thirty-six hours. Next, I checked the railroad station. There was a New York-bound train leaving at six a.m. with no Pullman cars, only coaches. I taxied to the rail depot. Then I slumped on a bench to wait for the train that would take eighteen long hours to reach New York.

I discovered why all forms of transportation were booked. Two troop ships had arrived in Miami from North Africa with 20,000 or more troops raring to go on leave. The train arrived loaded with soldiers with standing room only. I sat on my sea bag until we reached Atlanta, where many of them got off. I slumped into a seat and collapsed.

The coaches were old wooden cars with cane seats that reminded me of the midshipman train trip from Bucksport to 125th Street several years before. The cars were hot and unventilated. Open windows let in cinders and smoke to dirty us all.

I felt pretty lousy. Handling my own baggage and walking any distance caused my hands and feet to swell again. The hives reappeared and sweating didn't help.

Darkness became daylight and then darkness again. The hours seemed endless. The trip was an ordeal. We rolled into Washington, D.C. and had a twenty-minute stop. I took my baggage and went to the ticket counter and learned there was a train leaving for Boston in one hour. I booked a Pullman berth, crawled aboard and went to sleep. I never heard the train leave the station. The porter had to shake me when we arrived in Boston. I taxied from South Station to North and boarded the "milk train" to Portland.

I had kept a daily record of my temperature and ailments since Algiers, on the advice of the doctors there. I took these to my doctor in Portland. He made several tests and checked me over. He confirmed that I had a collagen disease. He said that not a great deal was known about it and he thought it would gradually pass. He was right, but it took almost a year before I was clear of it.

I tried earnestly to convince Connie that I thought we were foolish not to get married. World conditions were still uncertain and my future was unpredictable. I had no idea when I would be home again. She didn't want to take the chance of being expelled. She was more than halfway through her training and it didn't seem sensible to give it all up. We agreed we would arrange one more appointment with the superintendent of nurses to see if she would permit us to get married.

Before Connie's affiliation at the Concord State Hospital, those in her class had been given the opportunity to become Cadet Nurses in the Army Corps of Nurses. It was a government program that provided special nurse-cadet uniforms and $65 per month. Her whole class joined and by doing so, they agreed to remain in nursing for two years. It also made her obligated for active Army service after graduation. That is what troubled me.

The war in the Pacific was far from over, although our successes appeared to signal a victory. Losses during our island hopping were substantial. The expected invasion of Japan itself was predicted to be very costly. Medical facilities and nurses would be sorely needed. The prospect of Connie being drawn into the Army Nurses Corps looked quite probable to me.

I enrolled in a government-specialized training course at Chester, Pennsylvania. It was a three-month program in turbo-electric engineering that would qualify me for the new T-2 tankers being built. I found a room in a private home not far from the General Electric Training Center at Chester and settled in for three months of schooling. The swelling of my hands and feet kept occurring with a slight increase in temperature. Aspirin and a night's sleep usually quieted the problem for another day.

Classes were challenging. I dug in and found myself enjoying the learning process again. The class on electricity was rather involved in the study of atomic matter, neutrons, protons and the basic elements of energy. This was a new theory for me. Within a few weeks, it had a most significant meaning; President Harry Truman announced the bombing of Hiroshima with a new kind of atomic bomb. The war ended shortly after.

Following graduation I spent eight days in New York, checking in daily at the War Shipping Administration Office, expecting an assignment. On the eighth day, they ticketed four of us to New Orleans by Pullman. After a long two-day trip, we reported to the New Orleans office. The tanker they had assigned me had already been manned and departed. The other three guys were assigned ships and left. I checked into the "Carol," a seamen's hotel on suburban St. Charles Avenue and reported daily to the shipping office. For the next seventeen days, I checked, but still no assignment.

Finally I was sent to a new T-2 tanker being completed at the shipyard in Mobile, Alabama. The tanker was named the S. S. *Seneca Castle* and was at the outfitting pier at the shipyard across the bay. For fifteen days we ferried back and forth across the bay until the ship was finished. It gave me a chance to get acquainted with an entirely new and different engineering plant.

I signed on as third-assistant engineer with a first assistant's license rather than waiting for a better assignment. The crew came on board the day before we sailed and we took on stores, fuel and water.

The world was becoming normal again. Rationing and wartime restrictions were terminated. The boys were gradually returning home by planeload and shipload. The War Shipping Administration expected to announce a formula to release merchant sailors to civilian life. I was confident that I had served sufficient sea time to qualify for the first release. I was quite certain this trip would be my last, unless finding a job ashore proved difficult.

The thought of marriage was constantly on my mind. Thinking ahead became a preoccupation. What assets could I offer a potential employer? I turned possibilities over in my mind. I didn't worry about it. I just kept thinking.

By now I was very firm in wanting to settle down and begin my life anew. In less than a year, Connie would be graduating and, in one way or another, we were going to get married. I simply had to establish a livelihood and a security base. Some kind of job with a future was essential. I probably would have to seek employment in some mechanical engineering endeavor.

The space and accommodations on the *Seneca Castle* were large and luxurious compared to Liberty ships. It was indeed a substantial change. Once underway, she ran smooth as a top.

There was another significant difference. Although painted gray, she lacked gun tubs and the usual defensive armament and there was no armed guard crew assigned. The company's symbol was painted on her stack.

Six hours' sailing brought us up the ship canal to the Sinclair Refinery at Houston for loading. The following afternoon we steamed back down the ship canal with our destination Bayonne, New Jersey, and crossed the Gulf in glassy, calm water with gorgeous full moon overhead. Flying fish, porpoises and all kinds of bird and sea life amused us. We rounded Florida and sailed close to the coastline, arriving at Bayonne seven days later.

After we discharged our regular cargo of gasoline, we shifted across the bay to another terminal and loaded a full cargo of high octane aviation fuel. Our fourteen-day crossing to Dover, England was stormy and rough. With a pilot on board, we continued through recently swept mine fields off Holland and anchored for a day in Bremerhaven, Germany.

Destruction was evident there and several sunken vessels littered the harbor, including the prewar luxury liner, the *Bremen.* We moved up the Weser River to a small isolated petroleum depot at Farga and immediately began pumping cargo.

Our upriver passage took us directly past a huge, multi-storied, concrete submarine assembly building. It was visible from miles away. Repeated British air assaults had caused slight damage. Prefabricated submarine sections were joined within this huge structure and launched ready for service through its single riverside opening. It was an impressive structure and dominated the flat river plain.

Late that afternoon, three of us started out to see the town. A single road passed near the depot. It was chilly, dark and drizzly as we walked along. Eventually, we heard a vehicle approaching. It stopped and picked us up. Three of us squeezed into the rear of a Free French jeep. The soldier driving the jeep couldn't speak English. He dropped us off in the town of Blumenthal, after a lengthy ride.

Blumenthal was the headquarters of an American army division. The occupation troops were everywhere. We visited one of the large buildings where enlisted men were billeted. A new Enlisted Men's Service Club was opening that night and we were invited to join the celebration.

We were driven by jeep to a large hall crammed with Army people and blue with smoke. An orchestra was playing and waiters were barely able to make their way through the sea of bodies. We sat at a large round table with our Army hosts and ordered drinks. The hall was fully decorated. Conversation and laughter drowned out the entertainment.

Suddenly I noticed an Army captain with an Army nurse in tow, elbowing their way through the crowd. It was a strange feeling to see a person I knew. He was a high school acquaintance in the class ahead of me. I stood and yelled as loudly as I could. I finally caught his attention and they gradually worked their way to our table. He introduced me to the nurse. They were engaged to be married. We talked and got up-to-date on recent events. I invited the two of them to join us the next day for Thanksgiving dinner aboard ship. They accepted.

We left the Enlisted Men's Club at the invitation of two Army majors and were driven to an officer's olub several miles away. We entered an elegant chateau with towers, a grand portico entrance and a long driveway surrounded by lawns and gardens. It was a huge, former estate with many rooms, high ceilings, old world decorations and framed wall paintings. A curved marble staircase dominated the entrance area. Two large rooms led off on either side. More activity appeared to be at our right, so we walked in.

A small band was playing and the central area was utilized by a dozen couples dancing. We danced with local girls for several sets and nursed a drink or two. We were driven back after midnight to our remote tie-up at the petroleum depot. It was an interesting experience which left us with the impression that our occupation forces were really living it up in great style. Perhaps they had earned it.

The following afternoon, my former school friend and his bride-to-be came on board and joined us for Thanksgiving dinner.Following dinner, I gave them a tour through the ship. An hour following their departure, we steamed down the river for our return voyage to the states. We received mail as we slowed down to swap pilots at Bremerhaven. Information arrived that I was qualified to become a civilian.

Our voyage back to the states was as stormy and uncomfortable as our trip over. Twice we had to drop our speed and alter our course because of severe weather. I began packing three days from Galveston and, when we docked, I was ready to leave the minute we were paid off. My ills and aches were mostly memories. On occasion I had a slight recurrence, but generally felt good.

An era was ending. Sea life was behind me. I was now part of a large group of unemployed. The future had to be planned, but I was optimistic.[1] Christmas was just ahead. Certainly Santa Claus would be good to us this year. My twenty-one year old mind was filled with cheerful thoughts. My nautical life was over.

A slight regret twinged my mind. The sea had made a profound impression on me. Its fury and its grandeur, its peace and its ever changing face were firmly etched in my mind.

Those who live ashore have no idea of the beauty, the tranquility and the inner satisfaction the oceans provide. There are as close to creation as you can get and I am not surprised that sailors generally have a deep faith.

[1] Connie Canning and George Elliott were married on Washington's Birthday, 1946. Three weeks later George joined the staff of the advertising department of the Portland Newspapers. Recalled to active duty the Korean War, he served on a destroyer in the Atlantic. Mustered out, he returned to the Portland Newspapers and left in 1964 to form his own advertising agency. Today, semi-retired, Connie and George live in a contemporary home on a lake in Western Maine.

Bethell, Nicholas. *The Last Secret*. New York: Basic Books, 1974.

Boldov, A.V. Editor. *Northern Convoy: Research, Reminiscences, Documents*. Moscow: Nauka, 1994.

Bunker, John. *Liberty Ships: The Ugly Ducklings of World War II*. Annapolis: Naval Institute Press, 1972.

Garlinksi, Jozef. *The Enigma War*. New York: Scribner, 1980.

Elliott, George. *Wartime Diary*. Unpublished: 1943-45.

Gleichauf, Justin F. *Unsung Heros*. Annapolis: Naval Institute Press, 1990.

Hoehling, A.A. *The Fighting Liberty Ships: A Memoir*. Kent, OH: Kent State University Press, 1990.

Hoyt, Edwin P. *U-Boats Offshore*. New York: McGraw Hill, 1986.

Kemp, Paul. *Convoy!: Drama In Arctic Waters*. London: Arms & Armour, 1993.

Lewin, Ronald. *Ultra Goes To War*. New York: McGraw Hill, 1978.

Middlebrook, Martin. *Convoy*. New York: Morrow, 1977.

Morison, Samuel Eliot. *The Atlantic Battle Won, May 1943-May 1945*, Vol. 10, History of Naval Operations in World War II. Boston: Little-Brown, 1956.

— *The Battle of the Atlantic , September 1939-May 1943*, Vol. 1, History of Naval Operations in WorldWarII. Boston: Little-Brown, 1956.

Rohwer, Jürgen and Hümmelchen, Gerhards. *Chronology of the War At Sea 1939-1945: The Naval History of World War II*. Annapolis: Naval Institute Press, 1992.

Roskill, S.W., Captain. *The Offensive*. Volume 3,The War At Sea 1939-1945. London: Her Majesty's Stationary Office, 1961.

Schofield, Brian Bentham. *The Russian Convoys*. Philadelphia: Dufour Editions, 1964.

Sulzberger, C.L. *American Heritage Picture History of World War II*. New York: Simon and Schuster, 1966.

Tarrant, V. E. *The Last Year Of The Kriegsmarine*. Annapolis: Naval Institute Press, 1993.

INDEX

Liberty Ships Eastward was set in 12 point Goudy by Adobe. It was printed on 60 lb. Glatfelter Supple Opaque Recycled by Thomson-Shore, Inc., Dexter, Michigan. The book was designed and published by The Provincial Press, Cape Elizabeth, Maine